SUFFOLK FOR EVER

SUFFOLK FOR EVER

Edited by
Celia Jennings

Photographs by
Julia Hedgecoe

The Alastair Press

Published by
The Alastair Press
2 Hatter Street
Bury St Edmunds
Suffolk

First published in 1989

This book is published to mark the Diamond Jubilee
of the Suffolk Preservation Society.
1929–1989

ISBN 1 870567 70 6

Cover photograph: Stoke-by-Nayland
by Julia Hedgecoe

Photoset by Rowland Phototypesetting Ltd
Bury St Edmunds, Suffolk
Printed in Great Britain by
St Edmundsbury Press Ltd
Bury St Edmunds, Suffolk

Contents

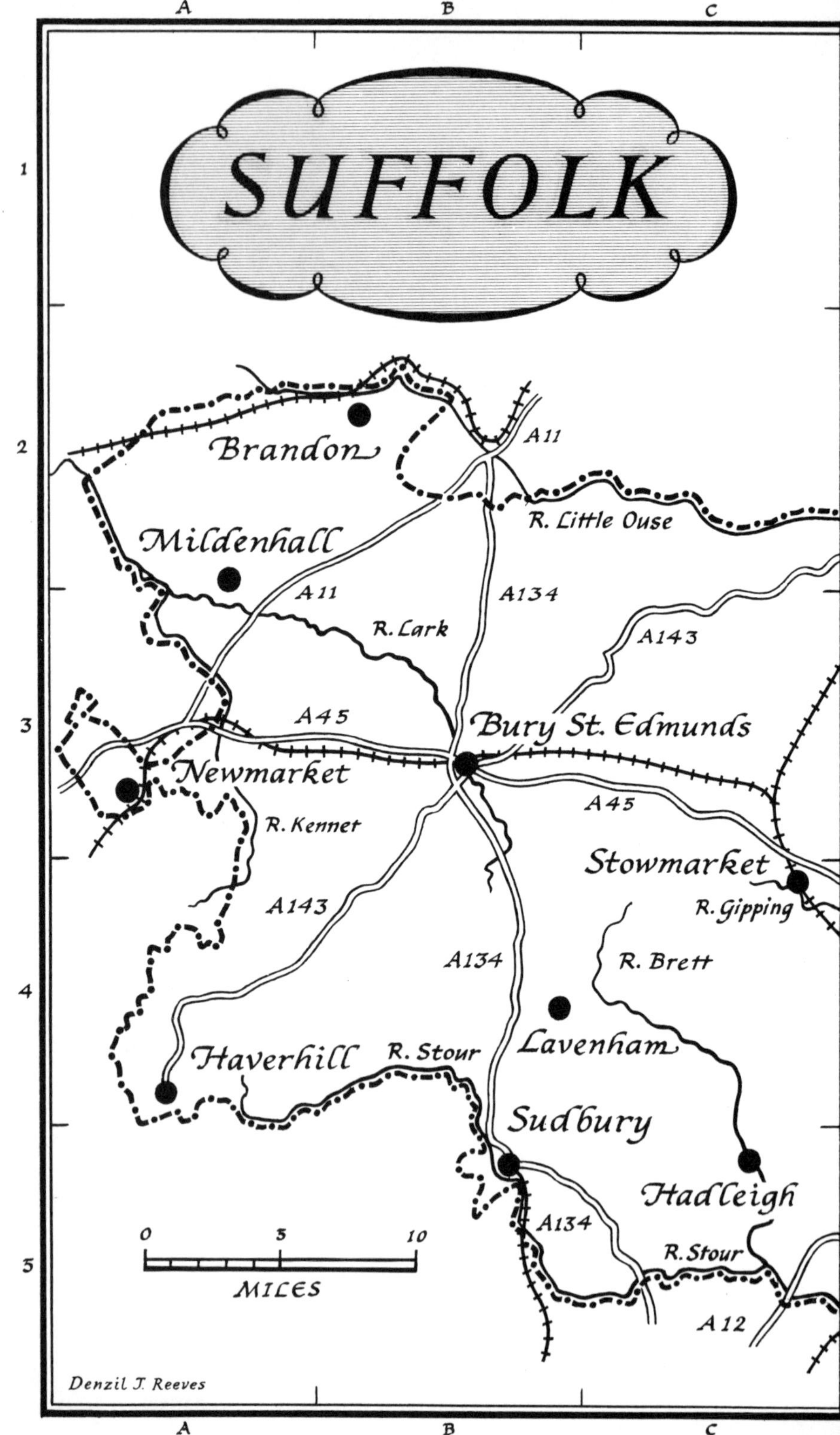
SUFFOLK
A
B
C
1
2
3
4
5
Brandon
A11
Mildenhall
R. Little Ouse
A11
A134
R. Lark
A143
A45
Bury St. Edmunds
Newmarket
A45
R. Kennet
Stowmarket
R. Gipping
A143
A134
R. Brett
Lavenham
Haverhill
R. Stour
Sudbury
Hadleigh
A134
0
5
10
MILES
R. Stour
A12
Denzil J. Reeves

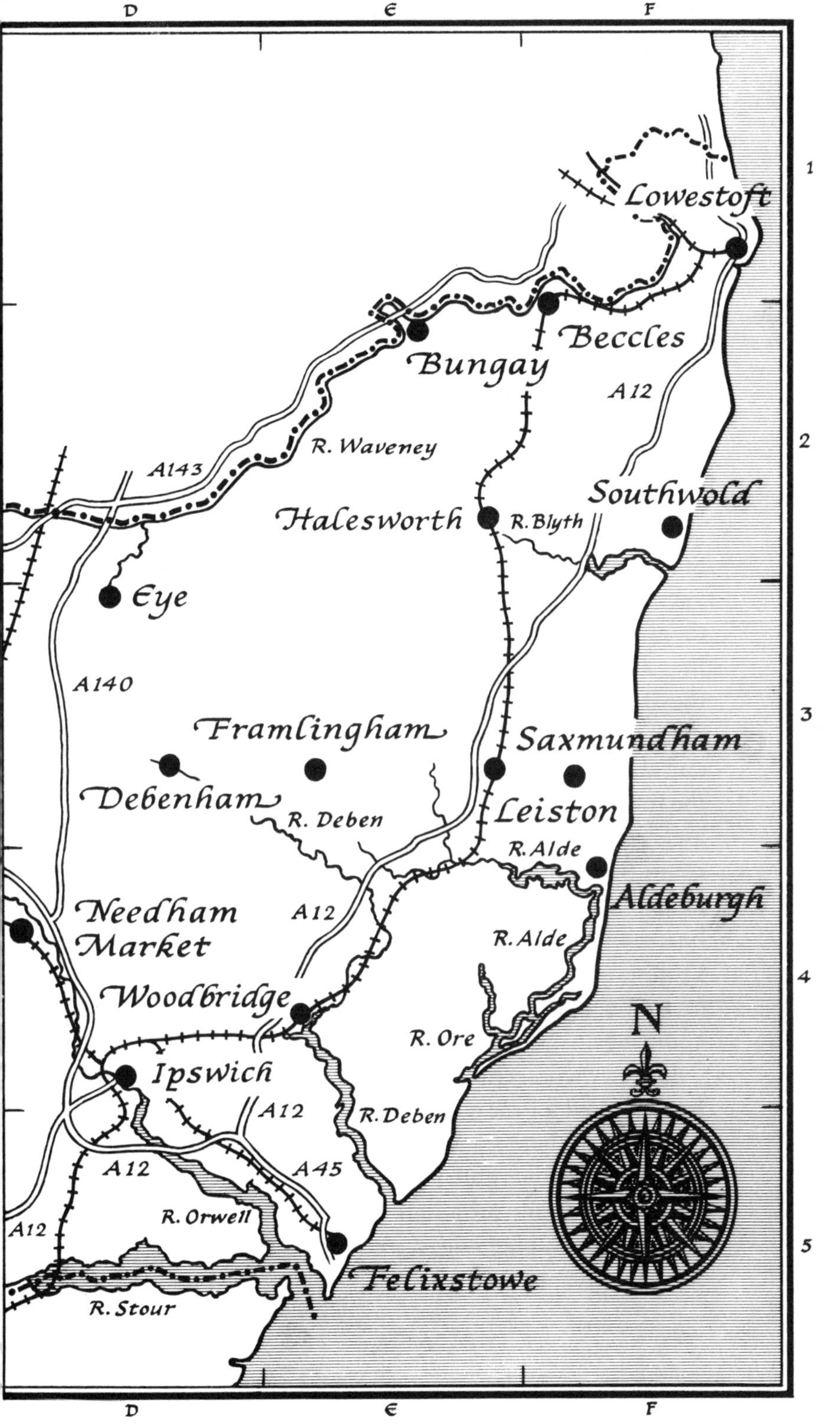
D
E
F
1
2
3
4
5
Lowestoft
Beccles
Bungay
A12
R. Waveney
A143
Southwold
Halesworth
R. Blyth
Eye
A140
Framlingham
Saxmundham
Debenham
Leiston
R. Deben
R. Alde
Aldeburgh
Needham
Market
A12
R. Alde
Woodbridge
N
R. Ore
Ipswich
A12
R. Deben
A12
A45
R. Orwell
A12
Felixstowe
R. Stour

Introduction

Celia Jennings

Suffolk for ever. The cord of hope that binds together these very diverse essays on a county which has subtly invaded the affections of this very diverse group of writers. Whether they are native-born or have settled in Suffolk later on in life they all have this in common, the conviction that while change is inevitable, *somehow* Suffolk's understated, elusive and above all unpretentious character should continue into the future. The ways in which each author views the future are very different, probably if they were all in the same room there might very well be a certain amount of good-natured argument; but on paper they have been given their heads, and if what they have to say provokes the reader into protest, so much the better, for no discussion of conservation is of any use if it is too bland, too polite, too complacent.

Indeed there seems little to be complacent about. Suffolk is earmarked for the building of 42,000 new houses by 1996, nearly all of them for what are politely termed 'incomers'. In 1989 the Government is expected to introduce a White Paper containing proposals to bring about a momentous change in the planning system, the abolition of County Structure Plans.

In spite of their many deficiencies these plans and their immediate predecessors, the County Development plans, have up to now provided a framework for a reasonably balanced development of the county and given conservation bodies a basis on which to fight against insensitive schemes. From now on the government's aim is to strengthen local responsibility for planning by transferring the power to make decisions almost wholly to the district councils and to reduce the influence of county councils. On the face of it there seems much to recommend this idea, but the hard fact is that few Suffolk local councils are sufficiently far advanced with their District Plans to be able to exercise careful control over the great pressure for development that is bombarding the county. There will inevitably be noticeable inconsistencies from district to district of a kind that the County Structure Plan is able to prevent.

With many of its powers reduced the County Council would undoubtedly lose some of its manpower, mainly, it is feared, those people who are concerned with what are sometimes seen as the non-essentials of the system – the many excellent services giving conservation help and advice and co-ordinating practical enhancement programmes. This cannot fail to detract from the character of Suffolk as a whole.

The loss of the County Structure Plan, should this come about, is perhaps more to be regretted in Suffolk than anywhere else, for the pioneering scheme from which all these plans came was produced here in 1935 when Patrick Abercrombie undertook a Regional Planning Scheme for East Suffolk, at the instigation of the Suffolk Preservation Society, the first of such documents in the whole of England. Abercrombie, later knighted for his influential work, is still one of the most highly respected names in the history of planning.

Ten years ago I was completing my research on a book on

the history of conservation in Suffolk over the preceding fifty years. Looking back I am astonished at how confident I felt about the outlook for Suffolk in the future. Of course the planning system was far from perfect. The fully justified worries about Sizewell B had already begun, population growth was even then well above the national average, there were serious worries that certain features in the landscape, hedgerows and rivers among them, were being ignored in the Structure Plan. But alongside these imperfections there were enormous improvements in the understanding of the county's architectural traditions and a phenomenal new interest in the natural environment. There was a real atmosphere of new confidence that the miserable, destructive decade of the 1960s was now publicly recognized as an unrepeatable mistake and that, however slowly, a better relationship was being established between the conservationists and the planners. Now many of the gains of these last few years may very well disappear. In an effort to reduce bureaucracy the safeguards that we almost take for granted are being eroded.

I think it would be true to say that in the last year or two public respect for the planning system, never very high, has plummeted. Everyone now knows that district councils, with their limited funding and enormous work-load caused by the huge increase in planning applications, are extremely reluctant to refuse planning permission if they believe they will be challenged at a public inquiry. Only in very exceptional cases, where an ancient monument or some other outstanding designation almost guarantees them victory will they take the risk. No wonder, as the bewildered residents watch the bulldozers moving in to flatten the banks of yet another green lane, that the general feeling is of despair and apathy. No wonder ordinary people without vested interest in the land look forward with dread to the relaxation of restraints on development of agricultural land taken out of production. No wonder those of us who remember the '60s look anxiously at every plot of land with access to the road, waiting for the day when we see the man with an acquisitive gleam in his eye and a tape measure in his hand.

But surely it can't all be doom and gloom? This book is called *Suffolk For Ever*, not *The Death of Suffolk*. Well, of course it isn't. There are innumerable hopeful signs and any number of positive things being done, many of them reflected in this book. In the first place Suffolk County Council has initiated some excellent schemes to improve the environment. A spectacular success has been the Dedham Vale Project, a joint enterprise between the county councils of Suffolk and Essex, the Countryside Commission and three district councils. The decaying landscape of the vale has been revitalized with tree-planting, the pollarding of the old willows, the restoration of the river banks and footpaths and a programme of efficient landscape management.

There has been a notable contribution to the countryside by enlightened Suffolk farmers, not nearly enough yet of course, but a sufficient number to show that it is still possible to run a profitable farm without damaging the landscape.

In the architectural field the Suffolk Historic Churches Trust has made a huge contribution to the maintenance of some of the most important features of the Suffolk scene. One has only to look, too, at the great advances in the understanding of the county's timber-framed buildings over the last twenty years. The two or three dedicated people who revived the interest in the vernacular style have now been joined by many younger ones whose knowledge of their own particular discipline is astonishing. Probably the most useful result of the new popularity of Suffolk is the revitalisation of pretty well every timber-framed house that still has part of its frame standing. Only a short time ago it was possible to see a potentially beautiful house standing derelict for years on end; now the picture is quite different.

Sadly the conversion of some of them is poorly done and would benefit from the advice of one of the many experts, but at least they have been saved, even if the land surrounding them has been sold off for new houses of the now almost inevitable standard design. Raw-looking pantiles, paying lip service to the vernacular, the deadly brown-stained mass-produced window frames, cement rendering, sometimes even the return of black nailed-on strips of timber. Commonest of all is the return of ornamental brick-work; quite reasonable in a place like Leiston, which has genuine Victorian examples of a similar style, but one sees dozens of these variegated brick buildings being hastily constructed in the most unlikely places – small villages even, where they look peculiarly alien. 'Developers' Vernacular' is nothing new, but the latest absurdities include bogus maltings and fake mill buildings, presumably attempts to placate the critics of urban buildings in rural surroundings.

Over twenty years ago, Norman Scarfe in his evidence to the Public Inquiry on the Shankland-Cox plan for Ipswich made an energetic plea for the public to become involved in the future of Suffolk. It has been quoted before, but is worth repeating, as it seems even more relevant today in a county that is under considerable stress.

> . . . the problems of preserving the character of the familiar environment, to ensure a proper continuity between past, present and future, are so many of them of a kind that have been given virtually no *professional* study. There are professional economists, planners, agriculturalists, but there are no *professional inhabitants*, no professional students of this particular human environment. But this does not exonerate any of us from the duty to the existing inhabitants of Suffolk to try to preserve at the very least, the best things in the world that they are used to and feel at home in.

This concept of the 'professional inhabitants' is now gradually coming into being. Never before have there been so many people eager to learn about the ecology and the history of Suffolk. Lectures, weekend and extra-mural courses, guided tours, have over the last few years made a massive contribution to the deepening understanding of the county. What was once the preserve of the butterfly collector or the antiquarian clergyman now occupies countless amateurs (in the best sense of that word). It must surely be true to say that there are now hundreds more of Suffolk's inhabitants who understand the historic landscape; why the roads in East Suffolk are so incredibly tortuous, why the small medieval farmhouses are dotted about in the fields wherever one looks, why so many parishes are composed of a series of straggling hamlets intersected by tracts of open country. These are the people who should be taking part in the discussions on the siting and design of new housing, not just the chap who knows the difference between good and bad house design (and there are few enough of those). But to harness these people into an effective body, to persuade them to give up their time to what is often an utterly tedious series of meetings is a problem which even the best of the many excellent amenity societies finds difficult.

The problem is to marshal the forces before it is too late. Over the past few decades it has been almost impossible to persuade the Suffolk resident that new building on a large scale brings no benefit to local traders or even guarantees that the village school will remain viable. Only after the village had doubled in size would the shopkeepers realize that the majority of newcomers did most of their shopping at out-of-town supermarkets. Many of these newcomers came to Suffolk to retire, and those who had children of school age, while they may have patronised the primary school where there was one, seemed to be less willing to entrust their children to Suffolk's often excellent High Schools. Over-development coupled with stagnation seems a strange paradox, but it is an all-too-familiar phenomenon in Suffolk today.

There *are* signs I believe that Suffolk is waking up to the dangers of over-development. It is not that the present residents are indiscriminately hostile to 'foreigners'. Many of them are after all, incomers themselves. Most Suffolk people are welcoming if undemonstrative; as one Orford man said 'I don't mind who comes to this place as long as they contribute something to its life'. This year for the first time, I have found born-and-bred Suffolk villagers prepared to write to a district council to defend some cherished view or some area that they have known and loved since childhood. But the onslaughts continue, more and more time is taken up with letter-writing and unless the people of Suffolk and those in counties similarly under threat can press for and get major changes in planning legislation, in less than twenty years much of Suffolk will be unrecognizable, for there are signs that even higher rates of immigration are being expected after 1996.

Or so we now think. One of the pleasantest aspects of planning forecasts is that they are so often wrong. The 1970 Strategic Plan for the South East seems to have overestimated the actual population growth in the area by something like two-thirds. Forecasting is a notoriously unreliable business. Fifteen years ago the Anglian Water Authority, with the enthusiastic support of some local farmers, drew up a monstrous plan to convert the Dedham Vale water meadows to arable; part of a 'rationalisation' scheme which included embanking the River Stour and drastically altering the very fields that Constable made world-famous. At a conference called to attempt to reconcile the interests of the authority, the farmers, conservationists and lovers of Constable Country someone questioned whether there was sufficient evidence to suggest that arable crops were always going to be as profitable as they then were. Shock and horror was expressed that anyone should raise such a heretical point – the world would always need cereal crops. Had the scheme gone ahead what would have happened now? Would the farmers have been willing to reinstate the water meadows, had it been possible to do so? How amazed these same farmers would have been, even so short a time ago, to be told of some of the crops they would now be experimenting with. Before the A12 was made into a dual-carriageway at Stratford St. Mary I remember seeing flax growing wild by the roadside, the remnants of the 1840s when Stratford Mill had been converted to produce linseed oil. This year along the Stour Valley I have seen wonderful expanses of blue, presumably being grown for the same purpose. We have become accustomed to oil-seed rape. Sunflowers and evening primrose may very well become an equally familiar sight.

We should surely be thankful that some of our farmers are prepared to try out new crops. With the present government's enthusiasm for the promotion of tourism our next great battle may be with the creation of theme parks and holiday villages. Marinas competing with bird life all round the coast, golf all the way from Lavenham to Bury, the commercialisation of some of the greatest of the churches – this, though admittedly for the upkeep of the building, is already happening in one of the most famous, with piped sacred music and an unacceptable amount of cheap souvenirs – a creation of a kind of Suffolk That Never Was, feeding off the more easily assimilated aspects of the county's past, all this adds up to the trivialisation of its elusive charm and its history of independence from London. For though it is such a short distance from the capital Suffolk has not yet been assimilated into the London orbit, as the Home Counties already were by the beginning of the

Second World War. Though we can no longer quite claim, as Golding Constable did to his son John, that as we approach Stratford St. Mary along the A12 from Essex we can 'perceive a change in the air', there is still a distinct identity which makes Suffolk more than a place with desirable houses and pretty country. One need look no further than the photographs in this book to begin to understand some of the qualities of its landscape, its buildings and its people which make it unique.

Its people. The one ingredient that cannot be protected by pressure groups or local societies. If Suffolk is to retain any of its special character, surely it must keep, as well as its landscape, churches, houses and wildlife, a reasonable balance between new-comers and those who were born and bred here. The problems of young people unable to afford to remain in their native towns and villages as property prices rise are now being recognized by Central Government and by parish councils. But progress towards providing reasonably priced housing for the local community is slow. Speculative builders are not interested in such an unprofitable market and the artificially high price of land which they create means that suitable sites for local needs are almost impossible to find. There is surely a case for parish councils to have greater statutory powers and to be able to draw up their own Village Plans, ideally in conjunction with 'professional inhabitants' who understand each village's special character – historians, naturalists, geographers, archaeologists – for many of the mistakes in our villages occur through a lack of understanding rather than by inbred insensitivity.

Perhaps speculative builders, instead of merely being given licence to build because no-one can prove an environmentally sound reason why they should not, should be required to prove an actual *local* need, not based simply on a set of figures from some planning forecast.

Above all, perhaps, before the century is out, we shall have to abandon the ever-diminishing dividing lines between all our county environmental organizations and come together in one huge pressure group. There would be much sadness, much nostalgia for the long and distinguished history of some of them, but if we really do want 'Suffolk for ever' we may have to set aside some of our emotional attachments, join forces and bring our views unequivocally to the attention of the people who hold the key to Suffolk's destiny.

David Dymond was born in Northampton but having spent most of his boyhood in Devonshire regards himself as a West Country man. After graduating with a history degree from London University, he became a professional archaeologist with the Royal Commission on Historical Monuments, based on the city of York and working on the field monuments of northern England. In 1965 he was appointed Resident Tutor in Suffolk for the Board of Extra-Mural Studies of the University of Cambridge, and shortly after became a member of St. John's College. Having taken to life in Suffolk, and married a girl from a Norfolk farming family, he sees no reason to contemplate leaving East Anglia in this lifetime. His main research interest is the study of local and regional history, particularly the life of Suffolk's rural communities. He has taught adult classes from Mildenhall to Westleton, and from Botesdale to East Bergholt, and become involved with many groups and individuals working on their own localities. Among his publications are *Archaeology and History* (1974), *Writing Local History* (1981), *The Norfolk Landscape* (1985) and *A History of Suffolk* (with Peter Northeast, 1985). The Dymonds have lived for nineteen years in a late-fifteenth century house in the village of Stanton; recently they moved to a converted pub (early-fourteenth century in part!) in Bury St. Edmunds.

The Landscape

David Dymond

As a migrant from the 'Shires' I have dubious qualifications for writing this chapter, for I arrived in Suffolk only 23 years ago and previously lived in faraway Yorkshire, Surrey, Devon and Northamptonshire. However, I can at least speak with the enthusiasm of a newcomer and convert who has fallen under the spell of Suffolk, and believes it to be one of the most fascinating counties in England, not least in its rich but unpretentious countryside.

The natural landscape of Suffolk is, before all else, undramatic and soft. This is not a county of grand vistas as from Hay Tor on Dartmoor, the Wrekin in Shropshire or Sutton Bank in Yorkshire. Admittedly, a few long views can be found. Many of us, for example, have enjoyed that curving sweep of shingled coastline from the cliff at Dunwich; or have gazed admiringly from Warren Hill on the edge of Newmarket, across intensively farmed fens towards the silver-tipped silhouette of Ely Cathedral. In general, however, the absence of mountains, great ranges of hills and dramatic escarpments means that panoramas are rare. When walking or driving through Suffolk, one does not normally see further than three miles, and often less than one mile. As a result the view is constantly changing, and changing totally, in a way that does not happen when one walks, for instance, along Wensleydale or on the slopes of Helvellyn. Visibility of course changes with the seasons, and one of the delights of walking in Suffolk during winter is to see something which is normally masked by leaves. But the range is nearly always fairly short, and the view usually enclosed by nearby ridges, hills or simply trees. Beyond that limited horizon our eyes are launched into the vast East Anglian sky where mountainous clouds often, if only fleetingly, display all the breadth and majesty which are lacking in the gentle scene below.

In fact, the natural undulations of the landscape are often so subtle that many visitors, even residents, are not even conscious of them. They write off Suffolk as 'flat', as Noel Coward did Norfolk. Of course, the county does have its flat plateaux, around Mendlesham airfield for instance, but many of us don't notice how frequently we climb out of a village, and over a ridge before dropping down to the next village, just as one does, but more laboriously, in Devon or Westmorland. And as we hurtle in top gear along the A45, many of us are not aware of crossing that highly significant watershed by Haughley Park, which divides the eastern part of Suffolk draining towards the North Sea from the western part draining towards the Wash.

A very important consequence of the small-scale, intimate character of the natural countryside is that certain features which would be overshadowed or lost in grander landscapes gain a special prominence in Suffolk: for example, church towers, woods, hedgerows, individual trees, barns, silos, battery-houses, lines of pylons. In this relatively soft fertile region which for well over a thousand years has been densely settled and intensively farmed, virtually everything, including the woods and heaths, is made by man, or determined by him, for good economic and functional reasons. In no other county of England is man's contribution so important visually, whatever its character or date.

Its geological evolution has given Suffolk a considerable variety of soils. Nearly all these, with the exception of some wet areas, are cultivable (though, interestingly, less than 2% is classified Grade 1). These soils have given rise to three main landscapes which we normally call the Breckland, the Sandlings, and central or High Suffolk. The Breckland in the north-west is an area of light sandy soils, much of it traditionally heathland and rabbit warren. In the nineteenth century it was largely redesigned into the present pattern of large, rectangular fields, plantations and tree belts. The Sandlings along the Suffolk coast is another area of light land. For centuries dominated by heaths and marshes, it was steadily transformed, particularly during the last 200 years, by enclosure, reclamation and afforestation. The relatively sparse populations of both these regions are concentrated in villages along river valleys, or scattered in isolated farmhouses of fairly recent origin. High Suffolk covering over two-thirds of the entire county is a total contrast. It consists of heavier loams and sticky, glossy clays which originally supported thick oak forest. This landscape has extraordinary intricacy, which is reflected in thousands of minor place-names recorded in medieval documents, many no longer identifiable. It is densely settled with frequent villages, hamlets, moated manors and isolated farmsteads; around them until the mid-twentieth century were patches of woodland, meadow and commons interspersed with myriad fields, on average no more than four to seven acres, frequently irregular but sometimes planned, all enclosed by deep ditches and thick hedges.

Our appreciation of Suffolk has traditionally been influenced by the visions of painters like Constable, of poets like George Crabbe and of writers like Julian Tennyson, but we now have a new dimension which gives us a priceless advantage over our predecessors. Suffolk's landscape is now vastly more studied and better understood than it was, say, forty years ago. (Sadly, one major reason for this has been the constant threat of destruction.) Thanks to a whole array of modern academic and scientific specialists including geologists, geographers, botanists, historians, archaeologists and conservationists, we have acquired a deeper and more accurate knowledge of the distinctiveness of Suffolk, the natural inheritance of plant and animal life, the age and development of its various landscapes, and the subtle interplay of the natural and man-made. Over and over again, this work underlines how important is the dimension of *time*.

We know, for example, that most of the Breckland was effectively cleared of its natural woodland by 2000 BC, and that even the heaviest land had been substantially cleared and supported numerous farmsteads by Roman times. It has been shown that many parishes had higher populations in the early Middle Ages than they have today; that villages and hamlets have expanded, contracted and shifted their sites with bewildering frequency; and that thousands of abandoned farmsteads of medieval, late Saxon, Roman and prehistoric date litter the arable fields of Suffolk. We have good evidence to show that most of the clayland was enclosed by hedges and man-made ditches by 1600; that some of our parish boundaries have been stable since the Bronze Age; and that relatively small acreages of permanent woodland were managed since at least the Middle Ages to produce vast quantities of timber and coppice-wood. It is now being suggested that large areas of fields, tracks and boundaries still in use today, like those around the village of Yaxley, may have been laid out in Roman or late prehistoric times. Many hundreds of timber-framed houses surviving from the Middle Ages, often disguised by later alterations, have been recently recognised and recorded for the first time. These are merely a few examples of priceless new knowledge which must be incorporated in any future vision of the county, and must be used to rebut those ridiculous myths which still persist in some wayward minds (such as, 'all hedges are the result of Parliamentary enclosure, and are only 100–200 years old', or, 'Suffolk was mainly forest 600 years ago').

This new research shows that the landscape has, throughout its history, undergone frequent change – a fact that should influence our attitudes to modern problems and pressures. Witness the following description:

> 'The big straggling fences were grubbed up and the wide ditches filled in and replaced by narrow straight gulleys. Miles of wide grass verge beside the country roads were annexed by the adjacent landowners . . . Isolated trees in the hedgerows, many of them good oaks, were ruthlessly felled, and one of the few nice woods in our district was entirely grubbed up and transformed into corn land.'

This description of the country around Debenham refers not to the 1970s, as you might think, but to the 1860s! Nor was the nineteenth century the only period when major changes happened. Footpaths and rights-of-way have been lost and extinguished for many centuries, often in the creation of private parks. From at least the sixteenth until the end of the eighteenth century, the most important element in Suffolk farming was dairying, and the production of huge quantities of butter and cheese; some central parishes then had as much as 85% of their areas under grass. Further back in time, large numbers of woods mentioned in Domesday Book, particularly in the north-eastern quarter of the county, were cleared during the twelfth and thirteenth centuries. These and many other examples prove that each generation, in inheriting the landscape, has justifiably claimed the right to change it, using the technology and economic opportunities then available. Sometimes, however, farmers found it difficult to make a living, and were inclined to let nature make the changes. We should never forget that the 'gloriously untidy' Suffolk which Julian Tenyson so admired in 1939, with its 'overblown and unruly hedges', was the result of about 60 years of agricultural depression and neglect. So, the ever-patient, thin crust of soil has at different times been cleared, abandoned, ploughed, put down to grass, enclosed, emparked, drained, and regularly re-fashioned. It is vital that all of us who claim to be conservationists should never argue against change itself: what matters is the character, the effect and quality of change.

Just as important is the principle of continuity. When they modified their inheritance, former generations always left intact much of the earlier countryside because money, technology and time were limited. They did not obliterate or destroy on a large scale. Thus houses tended to be modernised rather than completely rebuilt; fields were made larger by throwing together two or more earlier fields, or made smaller by simple subdivision. When a wood was grubbed out or a common enclosed, its shape was still preserved by its ancient ditches, banks and hedgerows. This dynamic and subtle interplay of change and continuity makes the Suffolk landscape a wonderful record of human management, a document of great complexity for us to study, interpret and cherish.

During the Second World War, English farming entered another Golden Age which reached its peak in the 1970s and early '80s. This has been called the second Agricultural Revolution – actually, it's more like the 22nd! Aided by guaranteed prices and massive subsidies from the taxpayer, farming once again became profitable and highly successful. To produce as much home-grown food as possible, farmers were officially encouraged to increase their acreages, invest heavily, mechanize rapidly and use huge quantities of herbicides, pesticides and fertilisers. In 40 years the yields of crops have more than trebled, and are still improving annually by 2 to 3%. In Suffolk, the process of 'arabilisation' which began in the late eighteenth century has continued so that 83% of available land is now ploughed.

The effect of this revolution on the appearance of the countryside was dramatic, and will remain for all time. Farmers were exhorted to increase the sizes of their fields, grub out hedgerows, fill ditches, fell woods, under-drain, deep-cultivate, plough up pasture – all was grant-aided and completely free of planning controls. Furthermore, they were given no advice on how to distinguish between those features which could be sacrificed, and those which might have been retained for historical, biological, visual or recreational reasons. In fact, such reasons were not even regarded, officially, as relevant. The result was a haphazard, unsystematic dismantling of the traditional landscape, and destruction at a pace which was historically unprecedented. With the help of a new technology of earth-moving equipment and power-saws, the farming community in 40 years removed large parts of what their predecessors, by hand, had created over many centuries.

Surveys have produced some alarming statistics. In 60 years over 80% of Suffolk's coastal heaths have been destroyed, and 85% of the Breckland heaths. Most parishes in the county have lost 50% of the landscape features which they had in about 1840, and in some cases over 70%. In the ill-used parish of Tannington, 75% of the mileage of hedgerow has been grubbed out. And so on. The losses include all those fragile, historical features which are rich habitats and 'canals' of wildlife, but which, once lost, are difficult or impossible to replace: hedges, green lanes, hand-dug ditches, road-verges, ponds, medieval moats, woodland, ancient pollards. Over this traumatic period, many footpaths vanished; the field-gate became an endangered species; public roads turned into drains; natural streams were canalised; valleys were ploughed across; many traditional buildings lost their 'embowered' look. Above all, the scale of the landscape was frequently transformed and that feeling of enclosure which is vital to the character of Suffolk was destroyed. It is little wonder that, for some people, the plough is no longer a symbol of good husbandry but one of menace and destruction. What continually puzzles me is that this painful episode in our region's history has not been recorded more by local poets, artists and photographers. When the green in the centre of Honington village was enclosed in 1800, Nathaniel Bloomfield, Suffolk's equivalent of John Clare, burst into primitive but passionate verse:

While the Green, tho' but Daisies its boast,
Was free as the Flow'rs to the Bee;
In all seasons the Green we lov'd most,
Because on the Green we were free.

But where is the twentieth-century poet of Tannington, Mickfield or Ixworth?*

A strange imbalance can be seen between our attitudes to buildings, on the one hand, and to the farmed countryside, on the other. Think of the outrage if 70% or even 50% of the traditional houses of Lavenham, Chelsworth or Kersey had been swept away in 40 years! And remember, as John Popham has said, that 'all this happened in Britain, the nation whose planning system was the envy of the world';

* Since this chapter was written, I discover, to my embarrassment, that a poem was indeed written in 1971 about the parish of Tannington. It contains the lines:

'Now puny man
with ruthless might
has stripped you stark and bare.'

The author was Eileen Riley, who was reacting to the stimulus of European Conservation Year.

for two decades we didn't even recognise the problem, and then for a third decade merely argued about it. The tragedy is compounded by the fact that detailed guidelines could so easily have been officially recommended. For example, when five or even ten fields were thrown together, the impact could have been offset by maintaining or even strengthening the boundaries of the new, large field, but normally this was not even considered. Major linear features which traditionally defined and 'punctuated' Suffolk could have been given special protection: the ditches, hedges and verges alongside roads, parish boundaries which had been 'beaten' by local communities for a thousand years or more, and those ditches, hedges and scarps which for centuries marked different zones of land-use, for example around commons or at the sides of valleys large and small.

We all have our special 'horror stories' of the 1960s and '70s. One day, when washing-up at the sink, I saw a 300-year oak near my house sway and slowly topple. On rushing to the spot, I was told by two rather bovine operatives that the tree was in the way of a new powerline. In fact, the removal of one limb would have sufficed. In an adjoining parish on another occasion, I was just in time to see the last roots and logs carted away from a green lane called Peddars Way, a superb length of parish boundary which was probably a Roman road in origin. No doubt you, like me, avoid certain lengths of road as being too painful to drive on. I would rather go miles out of my way than take the B1123 between Metfield and Linstead, where it crosses a plateau denuded, first, by the creation of a wartime airfield and, secondly, by pitiless farming. With modern technology we can grub out a hedge in a day, demolish a building in a morning, and fell a tree in a few minutes, but do we really have the sensitivity and responsibility to wield that power?

These criticisms do not mean, of course, that destruction has been total. In fact, the landscape is now very uneven because farmers and landowners have, mercifully, varied greatly in their attitudes and policies. By merely crossing a road or ditch, we can pass from a bleak, soul-shrivelling scene created by someone who in the Middle Ages would have been punished by his manorial court for 'strip and waste', to the farmscape of a true 'custodian of the countryside' who has made plenty of changes but still retained important threads of continuity and a sense of enclosure. Can anyone prove that the latter has been less successful economically in the last 30 years, or can anyone doubt that he is better placed in the new environmentally-conscious agriculture which is just dawning?

Threats to the countryside have inevitably stimulated much protest in the last few decades. This has taken several forms: agonised letters to newspapers, seminars and public meetings, the lobbying of officials and politicians, and the founding of new societies and groups. Although many people have felt powerless, often unable to comment or intervene because destruction had happened so quickly and without warning, the expression of public concern has in some cases been followed by successful action. One thinks, for example, of the public inquiry which helped to save most of the Bradfield Woods. At that time the local authority seriously suggested that the centre of the woods might be grubbed out, providing a fringe of trees was left around the perimeter. Since then, the ecological value of ancient woodland has become much more generally recognised, and many woods have come under protection. Cowpasture Lane, an attractive green lane at Mellis which was originally an important medieval road, was saved by local outcry which led to the imposing of a Tree Preservation Order. Sizewell Belts, a biologically rich area of marshland and trees, was successfully defended by the Suffolk Preservation

Society as part of Britain's longest -running public inquiry.

Nor should we forget the contribution of the much-maligned planning profession, which has had to learn the wisdom of ages in one generation. Although under enormous pressure, planners have become stout defenders of the rural environment by advising farmers, offering grants, negotiating management agreements, improving public access, producing publications, and giving protection by certain statutory designations. Two excellent recent examples of their enterprise are the Habitat Survey master-minded by the County Council, and the Sandlings Project in which local authorities are working closely with conservation bodies to save and restore the remaining coastal heaths with their acid grassland, heathers and characteristic fauna including the stonechat, adder and silver-studded blue butterfly. In addition to this institutional and public enterprise, many individuals have also had great influence in Suffolk. It would be invidious to list names, but they include local government officers, practical conservationists, academics, civil servants, advisers, teachers and, be it noted, farmers and landowners. In the long term, all these efforts have undoubtedly contributed to a marked change of attitudes, as a glance at recent issues of *The Suffolk Farmer* will clearly show.

But the conservation movement carries grave disadvantages which have seriously limited its effectiveness. For example, voluntary and official bodies tend to have limited objectives, and do not always find liaison easy. Thus within Suffolk we have a county society for archaeology and history, another for wildlife and natural habitats, another concerned with footpaths, and the Suffolk Preservation Society (SPS) which from its foundation in 1929 has been mainly interested in the architectural heritage. But naturalists are not particularly inclined to confer with students of architecture, and *vice versa*. Members of the Farming and

Wildlife Advisory Group can show a touching innocence in matters historical, while members of the Suffolk Institute of Archaeology care little for fritillaries and avocets. Yet we all need each other desperately if the case for conservation is to be finally won. Those of us interested in historical, farmed landscapes need allies particularly among naturalists, because their subject has a markedly greater popular appeal. The Suffolk Institute of Archaeology has about 700 members, the Suffolk Preservation Society about 2200, but the Suffolk Wildlife Trust has over 10,000. These figures of course betray another weakness, that societies, even the largest, have limited memberships and are largely middle-class in composition. This weakens our claim to represent the population at large – something which it is vitally important for conservationists to emphasize, even if the masses don't yet seem to appreciate what is done in their name!

Even more damaging is what I call the 'oasis mentality'. By this, I mean that we all tend to fight for particular, outstanding features which may then be given special protection or 'designation'. Thus, we toss around terms like Scheduled Monument, Listed Building and Heritage Coast, or acronyms such as SSSI (Site of Special Scientific Interest), AONB (Area of Outstanding Natural Beauty), ESA (Environmentally Sensitive Area) or NNR (National Nature Reserve). The Sandlings provides a good example of the complications. It was made an AONB in 1969, and its Heritage Coast was designated in 1974; within its boundaries are three NNRs and thirteen SSSIs. All these devices are backed by legislation and have their undoubted uses. Yet by drawing attention to the best examples – the 'oases' – we leave unprotected the mass of ordinary, average places. As Common Ground say when encouraging local people in *every* parish to record and map *all* features which have value, 'everyday places desperately need our attention'.

What can we look forward to? As Asa Briggs told the SPS in 1979, 'the future is not what it used to be'. In the first place, the nature of farming is now changing radically. The Golden Age ended abruptly in 1985, just as earlier booms ended in 1921 and 1875. Because farmers have been far *too* successful and Europe now has large surpluses of food, subsidies have been cut and prices are now falling. Therefore, for the first time since about 1940, farmers' incomes are declining and so is the value of agricultural land. Moreover, farming investment has plummeted to its lowest level since the mid-1950s. Having been exhorted for decades to increase productivity, farmers are now advised to turn away from intensive methods and to find new sources of income. It must be stressed that this *volte-face* in farming policies has involved an amazing official conversion. THE MINISTRY OF AGRICULTURE HAS DISCOVERED THE ENVIRONMENT. By the Agriculture Act of 1986, the Ministry is now required not only to consider the promotion of stable and efficient farming, the economic and social interests of rural areas and public access and use, but also 'the conservation and enhancement of the natural beauty of the countryside'.

Farmers and their employees, now less than 5% of Suffolk's working population, face an uncertain and worrying future. They are confronted by many imponderables, but the situation is not without hope or opportunity. Some farmland will undoubtedly be sold for new housing, roads, industry and public utilities, simply because East Anglia is one of the fastest growing regions of Britain and under considerable economic pressure. Farming incomes may be in general decline but it seems unlikely that government, and indeed the public, would want to see agriculture slide back into the chronic depression which afflicted it before the Second World War. So much will depend on how the public money formerly spent on intensive agriculture is redeployed, that is, in establishing the right financial inducements to farm differently. In fact, new grants for new purposes are already available, and more are being discussed. For example, the Farm Diversification Grant Scheme (when will bureaucrats learn not to clang nouns together?) came into operation in January 1988.

Diversification could of course take many forms. The search is on for alternative crops and animal products, perhaps linked with the new desire for organically grown and 'healthier' food. More direct retailing from farms could result. Tourism might also provide opportunities, though many of us would be worried by a rash of motels, caravans and holiday-villages. More sporting and leisure facilities such as golf-courses, fishing lakes and shooting ranges could be provided on what is now farmland. These activities would naturally give the public more access than they enjoy at present. Suffolk is already noted for its 'horsiculture' and that could spread further. Of course conflicts of interest could easily arise, if the new changes are not properly planned. The mind boggles at the thought of horse-riders confronting motor-cyclists, or of ramblers flushing out infuriated ornithologists. Finally, more rewards should come from the continuing conversion of redundant farm-buildings. Here, one is not only thinking of converting barns into houses, but of the scope for accommodating new forms of small-scale business and industry (not so different from those which abounded in rural Suffolk in the seventeenth century).

To reduce agricultural production, the solution at present most favoured by the EEC and British government seems to be 'set-aside'. This means deliberately taking out of cultivation up to 20% of the land now ploughed. Much hinges on whether it should be voluntary or compulsory, and on the levels of compensation to be offered. Farmers who are members of the SPS have already said that the levels of compensation so far proposed will do 'little to tempt the average arable farmer'. Environmentally, a great danger is that the scheme could lead to even more intensive methods on the 80% of land *not* set-aside. In fact, some farmers are already increasing output to compensate for falling incomes. The Council for the Protection of Rural England (CPRE) favours 'extensification', that is, reducing output by reintroducing fallows, using fewer chemicals, or increasing the amount of spring-grown crops which generally yield less and do not require so much spraying. Certainly, such an approach would have a much broader effect on the landscape, and would help to reduce disquiet about the build-up of nitrates in underground water-supplies. It might also enable farmers to establish a much better relationship with the British public, who not only pay supporting taxes but who, as consumers, are steadily changing their eating habits and becoming ever more environmentally conscious.

For those of us concerned about the Suffolk landscape, the management of Environmentally Sensitive Areas is an encouraging portent for the future. An ESA is designated 'where farming methods have helped to create an exceptionally attractive landscape and valuable habitats for wildlife'. Suffolk now has three of these Areas wholly or partly within its boundaries: the Breckland, the Broads and Suffolk River Valleys. In return for grants, farmers can, quite voluntarily, contract for five years to farm and manage carefully defined areas in a particular way. Many admirable ingredients are there. The scheme encourages the planting of trees, and the creation of headlands around arable fields and other 'wildlife strips'; it controls the use of chemicals, and gives the chance to change land-use (for example, converting arable to pasture, or to heathland). In addition, it gives the opportunity of 'restoring' features in the landscape, based on what survives or once existed, like the gappy hedges which are commonplace in Suffolk today or the meadows where plant-communities need strengthening. This form of management has been described by the CPRE as a 'most valuable precedent'. It is indeed far superior to mere set-aside and, if extended, could reverse the destructive trends of recent decades.

The National Farmers' Union has always argued that its members are the natural 'custodians' or 'guardians' of the countryside – indeed they should be, because their predecessors created the English landscape. It is certainly reassuring that a high proportion of farmers have responded voluntarily to the offer of grants in local ESAs. On the other hand, many critics say that voluntaryism is not sufficient, and that it has signally failed during the last 40 years. They argue that planning controls should be introduced to cover farmland, just as they have applied to buildings and the fabric of our towns and villages for several decades. What, after all, is the essential difference between a medieval house and a medieval hedge? Are not both historical monuments, and should they not both be given statutory protection? It is worth remembering that when the Wildlife and Countryside Act was passed in 1981, the idea of imposing planning controls on farmland was rejected in Parliament by quite narrow votes. Apart from special designations of the sort outlined above, and the dubious device of Tree Preservation Orders, we still have no *general* controls over the farming landscape. We may yet see the use of both stick and carrot. Statutory planning controls, mainly to discipline the 'stripper and waster', could be combined with financial payments designed to attract large numbers of farmers into voluntary agreements.

The current, long-overdue emphasis on conservation has come about primarily because of financial and political pressures, though I believe that protest and public education have played their part too. At last the realization is dawning that modern technology and affluence carry awesome and inescapable responsibilities. In our heart of hearts, we know that farming and land-ownership must involve a sense of trusteeship for future generations, and for the community as a whole. We are part of a chain of history and, with a due sense of humility, have a duty to pass on an environment which, although changing, still remains varied, rich and stimulating. Our farming landscape is an irreplaceable national resource which deserves protection, careful study and sound management. If these attitudes prevail, the tax-paying public will surely be willing to pay the price both of promoting conservation and of sustaining the farming industry.

The ultimate practical test in our county will be the fate of High Suffolk. We already have an ESA for a few river valleys which penetrate that region, but by far the greatest part of the claylands covering about two-thirds of the entire county has no protection whatsoever. Here it is vital to preserve or to re-create a sense of linear diversity and enclosure, especially on the extensive plateaux which are in places very denuded and ecologically impoverished. This is the oldest and most fragile of our existing local landscapes, yet it is the most under threat and the least protected. Nothing indicates more clearly how far we still have to go.

David Barker was born at Hall Farm, Langham near Bury St. Edmunds. He was educated at Moreton Hall and Culford School and obtained a National Diploma in Agriculture at Writtle, Essex.

He was chairman of the Suffolk Branch of the National Farmers Union 1985–86; chairman of the Suffolk Committee for 1989 Celebration of Food and Farming; vice-chairman of the Suffolk Farming and Wildlife Advisory Group and a council member of the Suffolk Agricultural Association and the Suffolk CLA Committee. He represents six Eastern counties on the National Farmers Union Central Finance and Organisation Committee.

He farms 1280 acres at Westhorpe, where he also lives, in partnership with his father and brother. Main crops: wheat, barley, grass seed, peas and beans with a pig herd.

A Suffolk Farming Revolution

David Barker

Since farming covers 90% of Suffolk's area, its significance to the county, its population, landscape and commerce far exceeds anything else. The farming industry will reflect decisions made in Westminster and Brussels, and the impact of political decisions far outweigh any made within the county. Whatever happens today or in the future, there is a very good chance that history will repeat itself.

During the twentieth century Suffolk farming has survived its golden ages and its periods of severe depression. Twice recession has been arrested by the conflict of world war, times when the maximum amount of food needed to be produced at home. In 1939 only 25% of the country's food requirements was produced at home, but this proportion has gradually increased ever since. After the Second World War all the British political parties agreed that the farming industry should never again be allowed to drift into the doldrums, and that food supplies should not be left at the mercy of foreign powers.

The 1947 Agriculture Act was the most significant piece of farming legislation this century. Its consequent effect upon Suffolk, its landscape and farming structure was dramatic. The Act was designed 'for the purpose of promoting and maintaining, by the provision of guaranteed prices and assured markets . . . a stable and efficient agricultural industry capable of producing such part of the nation's food and other agricultural produce as in the national interest it is desirable to produce in the United Kingdom'. The initial aim was to increase home food production by 20% in the next five years. By 1952 that target was increased to over 60% of the pre-war figure. In addition, government assisted agriculture by giving free advice from the Ministry of Agriculture.

The principle of the post-war policy was the guaranteed price. Each farmer would sell his produce as well as he could on the free market. The government would, when necessary, pay a direct sum to farmers (a subsidy), if the average market price fell below that guaranteed. Hence, if the guaranteed price of barley was £25 per tonne, and Farmer A sold for £24 and Farmer B sold for £22, the average trading price could be £23 and therefore a £2 subsidy would be paid to make up the difference.

An essential part of the system was the annual farm price review. Basically, government, farmers and the trade would meet to negotiate the guaranteed price level for the next year. In many ways this was an excellent system because if, for example, milk was in over-supply, the guaranteed price would be reduced and if pigs were in short supply, the guaranteed price could be increased to encourage greater production. It was an annual self-regulatory system of farm support that did not create surpluses but regulated supply to demand. Of course farmers were accused of being feather-bedded, but in fact, it provided a consumer subsidy and became known as the cheap food era. If the price of beef cattle traded below the guaranteed level, the consumer obtained the benefit of the cheaper beef while the producer retained a higher value.

Apart from supporting producer returns, the 1947 Act

sought to increase farm output by production grants. Grants were given for ploughing up old pasture to increase arable cultivation, for the liming of acid soils and drainage of wet and waterlogged areas. In each case government paid a proportion of the total cost. In France, on the other hand, the policy was to provide cheap credit, one purpose of which was to maintain existing farm holdings. When one looks at the dramatic decline in farm holdings in this country, one cannot help concluding that the French may have had a better system.

In 1950, Suffolk had 7,853 farm holdings, over three quarters of a million acres, and an average farm size of 95½ acres. This number actually increased by 1955 to 8,067, but since then it has gradually fallen to 6,534 (1966), 4,203 (1975), 3,669 (1985), by which time the average farm holding size had doubled to 204½ acres.

The post-war Farm Improvement Scheme helped provide modern farm buildings and equipment to effect greater farm efficiency during the rest of the century and beyond. In addition, the Ministry of Agriculture prevented development on good quality agricultural land, because it was in the national interest to maximise home food production.

This period after the war also saw the commencement of an agricultural revolution. It was a time when horse power made way for tractor power, and when jobs were transferred from farm to manufacturing industries. Many will have lived through this dramatic restructuring without realising that history would regard this as a revolution.

When I was a student in the late sixties, the great goal was increased production in order to save costly imports. Each month the most important statistic was not the number of people unemployed but the balance of trade figures, which too often reflected the United Kingdom's indebtedness to its trading partners. The increase in food production was vital to improving that situation.

Students left agricultural college with the Farm Improvement Scheme drummed into them. It is interesting to outline some of the main points:

a) Reclamation of waste land.
b) Removal of hedges and banks, filling in ditches, removal of boulders, tree roots and other obstructions to cultivation.
c) Land levelling work including filling in ponds and depressions which impede cultivation.

In later years when farmers were heavily criticised, no wonder many were confused! Having been encouraged by successive governments to increase output, they became accused of destroying the countryside. There is no doubt that in some areas the process was carried to the extreme, but at the time there were very few complaints. The tragedy was the loss of historic landscape features, removed in the name of progress; but the fact remains that no conservation criteria existed. In retrospect that was obviously a mistake. Government money should not have been used to remove ancient woodland, historic lanes or roadside features. It is a pity that the modern flail mower was not invented fifteen years sooner. Many features were removed because the labour no longer existed to manage them, and in later years the tasks could easily have been done by machine.

Throughout my two years of agricultural training the word 'conservation' was never mentioned. Some time was devoted to agricultural history, even horse husbandry, but any emphasis on environmental considerations was absent.

This agricultural revolution provided a gradual sustained increase in food production. Apart from enlarged fields, a big increase in the use of bagged fertiliser made a significant impact upon crop yields. It was not until the 1970s that spray chemicals to control diseases and insects became more widespread, and the herbicides to control weeds became more refined. Suffolk farms became much more specialised units rather than growing a range of crops and stocking many different farm animals. The trend was to grow crops best suited to the area and have one or possibly two livestock enterprises at the most. Indeed, many farms became purely arable units because the cost of re-equipping livestock buildings was substantial. It is instructive to quantify the changes in livestock and cropping.

In 1950 there were 37,642 dairy cows in Suffolk, by 1986 the figure was 17,751, (47% of 1950). What is not possible to ascertain is the number of farm holdings with dairy cows. My estimate would be some 40% had cows in 1950 but under 10% by 1986. Total cattle had reduced to 67.4% of the 1950's figure.

In 1950 there were 44,000 sheep on Suffolk farms, and by 1960 this figure had more than doubled. Twenty years later the number had dropped below the 1950 figure, but since then the support given to sheep producers by the EEC has brought an increase in flocks to over 51,000 by 1986.

The increased emphasis on pigs is revealed by the 1950s figure of 114,087. This figure doubled by 1955, more than trebled by 1965 and reached over half a million by 1970. Since then the total has increased to 617,000 by 1980, followed by a small decline in the next six years.

In many ways the poultry industry has changed more dramatically than anything else with 2.36 million birds spread across the county in 1950. This figure increased by a million in 1960, and a further million by 1970. It reached a peak of 5.69 million in 1975 since when the numbers have declined to below 5 million.

A significant change has been seen also on the machinery side. In 1950 there were still 12,312 horses kept on farms compared with under 8,000 three and four wheel tractors and 619 combines; (one to every 1,211 acres). Tractor hoes were outnumbered by horse hoes two to one.

The second and most important event for agriculture after the war was the UK membership of the Common Market in 1973, and with it came, more significantly, the Common Agricultural Policy (CAP). Before looking at the effects of the EEC, one must assess the reasoning behind it. Europe had just survived the traumas of war coupled with widespread starvation. European farming was fundamentally inefficient, ill-equipped and over-manned. Many small farmers were only producing at a basic subsistence level and rural incomes were well below those in industry. The principle of the EEC was to create a common priced agriculture, a social structure based upon family farms to provide stability of supply coupled with a maintenance of income. The Treaty of Rome, article 38, provides for a common market in agricultural products accompanied by a common agricultural policy amongst member states. Article 39 sought to increase agricultural production by promoting technical progress and to achieve a fair standard of living for the farming community. This meant an increase in the earnings of those engaged in agriculture. The aim was to stabilize markets and assure availability of food supplies to the consumer at a reasonable price.

The European system was fundamentally different from that which had been operating in the UK since 1947. The European philosophy was that consumers paid the full cost with taxpayers maintaining farm support by intervening to support farm prices. If, for example, the market price of wheat fell below the base price, farmers could sell it into member state stores at the base price. These became known as intervention stores. Sadly the principle of a common price has a variety of distortions because prices are based upon fixed 'green' rates of exchange for each national currency, which often may be different from the actual free market value of the currency. Throughout the UK's membership of the EEC the green pound (which provides the basis of home market prices) has been valued at a lower rate than sterling in the foreign exchange market, with the result that UK farmers have been at a substantial disadvantage compared with their European counterparts.

Because of the fluctuations in individual national currencies and the consequent distortions created to the base price, a system of MCAs (monetary compensatory amounts) was devised. The principle was that when the pound weakens it makes UK exports become more competitive, but to prevent this happening in farm produce MCAs are levied, in theory, to harmonise values by taxing exports and subsidising imports. The fundamental flaw of this complex system is that a common price no longer exists, resulting in wide differences between member states. The system is costly as well as containing a degree of fraud, particularly where a border such as Ireland allows illegal trade.

From an arable farmer's viewpoint, the early years of EEC membership were good because the UK reaped the benefit of higher returns with lower costs. It must be remembered that all the major political parties favoured EEC membership. The 1973 Heath government signed the Treaty of Rome and, despite subsequently 'renegotiating' our terms of entry, Harold Wilson's Labour administration asked for and received endorsement of our membership by way of a national referendum. I often become extremely irritated when journalists or politicians use the EEC as a means of attacking farming. It must be remembered that farmers did not ask for this change or the principles of the CAP. Many preferred (and still do), the system created by the 1947 Act.

Clearly one feature of the European farm system was political. Western governments were determined to provide better conditions for their rural communities than those in the Eastern bloc. This was underlined by the determination to ensure farmers living on the western side of the iron curtain displayed a superior life style to those eastern bloc farmers living just a short distance away. In addition France and Germany, mindful of their farmers' political influence, were determined to ensure an improvement in agricultural living standards.

In my view, the European system of farm support is inferior to that which was operating in the UK between 1947 and 1973. Certainly the aims are sound but when it was introduced no consideration was given to what would happen when the goal of self-sufficiency was reached. Inevitably, surplus stocks have to reach an embarrassing level before necessary and painful decisions are made. The great advantage of the pre-1973 support system in the UK was the annual adjustments. Food was not stockpiled and the consumers had the advantage of lower food prices. A good example was the graph of pig profitability quantified by the Cambridge University Pig Scheme. The period prior to 1973 showed a consistent level of margin between £10 and £20 over £100 output. After that the industry cycled dramatically with good years in 1975, 1978, and 1984, but quite dreadful years in 1974, 1977, 1983 and 1988.

The 1970s heralded dramatic changes. The plant breeder achieved unimaginable levels of yield. Tramlining (creating parallel, equidistant tracks through crops to enable machines to make accurate applications of sprays and fertiliser) became commonplace. Livestock production increased to new heights. Instead of sows producing two litters of eight pigs in the early sixties, twenty years later the norm was 2.2 litters of 10, a 40% improvement.

The most visual effect was the emergence of oilseed rape, grown to increase European production of cooking oils and margarines. Machinery increased from the 65 horsepower Fordson Major to the 100 horse power John Deeres. However the early benefits of the EEC were eroded by runaway inflation.

In many ways the 1970s epitomised the triumph of post war agriculture – enormous technical progress, incredible increase in production, vast productivity and a buoyant and largely successful farming industry saving the nation millions annually in food imports. Alongside the triumph was the sadness of the loss of many farm holdings and with them, many rural jobs and village traditions, and the disappearance of landscape features like old pastures. My own parish of Westhorpe lost its post office, shop and pub, joining the school which closed in the sixties. Yes, it will all be put down to progress, but I am not convinced that this is in fact true.

Surprisingly, the majority of field enlargements took place with relatively little controversy. The farms which had enlarged fields were regarded as the trendsetters of the 1970s. Later, they were to become the target of criticism in the 1980s. It must be remembered that these were what the efficient mechanical farms post-war policies were designed to achieve. Possibly more surprising is the fact that many farmers subsequently (mostly privately) regretted some of the hedge and pond removal that took place. This is certainly true in parts of our own farm. On the whole a sensible balance has been retained between modern farming and an attractive and diverse countryside. From a purely arable viewpoint, large fields have enormous advantages – less turning, few difficult corners, more even application rates and greater productivity.

However, the small well-hedged field also has its advantages – less wind problems, more benefit is available from useful predatory insects due to the field boundaries.

What is important and is often ignored for reasons of blind prejudice is the key role field sports have played in retaining the most attractive estates. The farm of the keen hunting and shooting enthusiast is the farm sustaining not just game birds and foxes, but a wide variety of other birds, mammals, insects, flora and fauna essential to countryside conservation. Fishing too, has also played its role in retaining and creating water areas on farms. The environmentally conscious farmer, too, is often much more selective in the use of agricultural sprays, ensuring pests are controlled with the least damage to beneficial insects necessary for the survival of young birds. Sadly, the exception to these beneficial activities is hare coursing, which is so often pursued by people with little or no regard to the traditions of the countryside or the people living in it.

The 1980s became a time of conflict in the countryside with public criticisms levelled particularly at hedge and woodland removal. Many farmers were both unhappy and bewildered, but looking back it may have been a good thing. It made farmers think hard before contemplating changes which, a few years earlier, would have been done without a second thought.

In Suffolk we have been most fortunate to have a County Council with the awareness and forethought to give a vital lead in providing both free advice and financial resources to help farmers make what was to many a difficult transition from farming for maximum production to farming in harmony with the environment. The County Council foresight was illustrated by its work in the New Agricultural Landscape Project which commenced in 1978. The project officer, Melinda Appleby, was funded by the Countryside Commission to work within six and later nine parishes north-east of Debenham. She was, no doubt, received with a degree of suspicion but gradually and successfully she won the confidence of the landowners and farmers in the area. The wider involvement of farming organisations like the Ministry of Agriculture, the National Farmers' Union and the Country Landowners' Association clearly helped and the results at the end of five years were really quite encouraging. Six of the woods reintroduced routine coppicing, and over 10,000 trees were planted, some 20 acres in blocks (i.e. future woodland). In addition, tagging of saplings in hedgerows will provide many future specimen trees. Around 12 moats and ponds were improved, and some farms in the area embarked upon whole farm conservation plans. There is no doubt that much of the project's success was due to Melinda Appleby. She was one of a team of County Council and District Council staff displaying knowledge and commitment to furthering the cause of nature conservation in Suffolk.

Some farmers are still reluctant to call in 'government' bodies for advice, hence the need for private consultation. The largest in Suffolk is the Farming and Wildlife Advisory Group (FWAG) which was formed nationally in 1969. The origins of Suffolk FWAG can be traced to Mr. Willie Kerr's farm at Letheringham in 1974, where a Suffolk Countryside Committee was formed representing all the main farming and conservation organisations. It was, in fact, the first county FWAG to be established. The organisation provides a forum for close contact between representatives of many organisations, ensuring barriers are broken down. The first Chairman was John Trist and the executive officer, Gordon Clarke. It was Gordon Clarke, formerly with the Ministry, who did an enormous amount of work, assembling consultants and generally achieving the acceptance that FWAG enjoys today. Mention should be made, too of the importance of the farmer members, in particular John Wilson of Ixworth Thorpe, whose outstanding contribution has been nationally recognised. Past winners of the FWAG competition have displayed the best of Suffolk agriculture. In 1985 John Horsman's farm at Cratfield achieved the ultimate accolade and was the winner of the Countrylife National Award. Also in 1985, Juliet Hawkins was appointed as FWAG's first full-time conservation adviser.

The conflict of the 1980s was typified by the *Daily*

Telegraph, in an article featuring the large fields at Ixworth, suggesting that they were the result of wholesale destruction of hedges whereas in fact they had been that size for generations. The farmers in that locality were so dismayed that they produced the most constructive possible response. The Stanton NFU survey 'The Countryside – FARMERS CARE TOO' was launched in 1985. It gave details of landscape features and conservation work over 126 out of 129 farms in the 28 parishes, which covered a fifty square mile area. To local people the survey only told them what they already knew. There were 2 square miles of woodland which was increasing. There were also 3 square miles of permanent pasture plus 1½ miles of temporary grass. Almost 74,000 trees had been planted in the previous 5 years, which indicated a tree planted for every 2 acres farmed every year. Some 372 miles of hedgerow existed in an area which some have claimed to be a prairie, and interestingly, there was a pond to every 68 acres of farmland. Perhaps of most interest were the wide variety of rare birds, plants and special habitats listed in the area, and the fact that otters had not just been released there but had actually bred successfully.

Certainly by all but the lunatic fringe the survey was well received. Farmers accept that a maverick minority may obtain the headlines but the vast majority are true custodians of the countryside. The beauty of Suffolk bears testimony to that. It is a tribute to their forefathers that today so many delight in and seek to conserve that remarkable countryside.

Gradually the barriers between farmers and conservationists have come down, not just because of a change in farmers' attitudes but because leaders of conservation organisations like the Suffolk Preservation Society and the Suffolk Wildlife Trust were equally determined to build bridges. The period of farmer-bashing highlighted a national debate on the Common Agricultural Policy. Sadly some television documentaries deliberately displayed a sinister motive to make the farmer unpopular in order to achieve political and agricultural change. Farmers recognise that the CAP and its policy of storing surplus food is in no-one's long term interest, but it is unfair to blame farmers for following a path created by political demands. The problem is that governments are often slow to react. For example, it was crazy to grant-aid one farmer to plant a hedge and also aid his neighbour to grub one out. Even more incredibly, in the 1970s one farmer could be paid a golden handshake to go out of milk production, while his neighbour could receive an EEC grant to increase production.

1984 was the year the EEC bubble burst. On April Fool's Day (many regard this as a highly appropriate date) the farm ministers introduced milk quotas to curtail the ever-increasing cost. The harvest of 1984 was the most remarkable ever in the UK around 26½ million tonnes of cereals. Land prices reached unsustainable heights. In many ways the 1980s provided the ultimate irony – land being 'set-aside' (being taken out of arable production to either fallow or non-agricultural use, to reduce the cost of storing surplus farm products). Farming has truly become a victim of its own success! Instead of being paid £12 per acre to plough up grass in 1970, a similar sum, in real terms, in 1987 of £80 an acre could be secured in order to retain pasture.

The major conversion of grassland was a critical factor in the gradual increase of the nitrate level in drinking water. Suffolk, fortunately, is not the worst affected area. Debates on this extremely complex subject are often ill informed. Sewage effluent and past farming practices as well as the use of inorganic fertiliser all have a significant bearing on the subject. The EEC imposed a 50 part per million standard for drinking water that was completely arbitrary and had no sound scientific base. Scaremongering stories about blue-baby syndrome (there have been no cases since 1972) and links with stomach cancer are not supported by medical evidence. The problem is that the European Parliament, (which some believe, with good reason, is a waste of time), makes decisions on emotive grounds and not on those with a sound scientific basis – a very dangerous practice!

Fortunately, the levels of nitrates in Suffolk show signs of levelling off; most recently farming advice has been tailored to reducing possible run-off. After all, nitrogen is as essential to the arable farmer as petrol is to the motorist, but it needs to be used with care and precision. Interestingly enough, less than one mile from my home is a borehole which consistently produces water of less than one part per million of nitrate.

By 1988 countryside conservation became an integral part of many farm operations. Indeed, it is a tribute to Suffolk farmers and conservation groups that central government has allocated considerable resources to environmental payments. However, farmers are understandably bewildered – after all, you may have an SSSI (Site of Special Scientific Interest) within an AONB (Area of Outstanding Natural Beauty), you may become involved with a Special Landscape Area and the Ministry of Agriculture may offer you an ESA Payment for an Environmentally Sensitive Area – it is no wonder that a degree of confusion reigns.

I believe that the ESA designation of the Suffolk River Valleys and in Breckland is excellent for Suffolk. It is, after all, a voluntary scheme but not surprisingly the interest shown by farmers has far exceeded expectations. The ESA principle is to achieve, under voluntary management agreements, a more flexible farming system. In the river valleys payments of between £28 and £72 per acre can be obtained to farm in an environmentally sensitive way. In Breckland the aim is to protect the heathland by grassland management (particularly grazing) and to encourage the continuation of the native Breckland wild flowers on field boundaries. The work of the Game Conservancy is significant and has shown a higher brood size of English partridge surviving in cereal fields with unsprayed headlands. The cereal 'weeds' provide an important food source not just for the young partridges but also for other birds, insects, butterflies and a wide range of wildlife. The ESA principle is a sound one and I believe all of Suffolk should become an Environmentally Sensitive Area, giving all farmers the chance to do more positive conservation work.

The New Farm Woodland Scheme is potentially significant. When one considers that the UK is only 10% self sufficient in timber, it must be right to encourage lowland woodland rather than the stupidity of covering attractive uplands with conifers. Occasionally some idiot will write a letter to the local paper suggesting that the new farm woodland scheme is like money growing on trees, but one must remember it takes 90 years to produce an oak gatepost and tree planting is an act of faith, with financial returns carried forward to one's great grandchildren. New woodland will only be planted in Suffolk given sensible incentives. The scheme will not just give grant aid to planting but annual payments for 10 to 40 years, according to the species planted. The main drawback is the need to plant a minimum of three hectares (7½ acres); thus with an average farm of 205 acres many smaller holdings will not have the scope to participate. The scheme will, I believe, be commended by future generations.

Whatever the future Suffolk has the finest soils, farm structure and back-up trade of any farmers in the world; given fair and equal treatment Suffolk farmers can take on and beat any in the world. The problem is that ever since 1974 successive British governments have used the artificial 'green' pound to undermine farmers' incomes. Despite the prospect of 1992, I will only believe in a free and fair market when it arrives. The problem has been agricultural since EEC support has become distanced from the market place. Pig keepers are an exception to this since they rely on little or no support.

From home production of only 25% of national food requirements in 1939, some fifty years later the proportion is over 80%. I have quantified the changes in farm holdings and livestock, but it is more difficult to compare the employment statistics. In 1950, the Suffolk farm labour force was 26,939 (22,152 full-time), but this figure, I believe, excluded farmers and their wives. In 1986 the total labour force, including farmers and wives, full and part-time employees was 14,266, of which 6,360 were full or regular part-time employees.

The most dramatic change has been in relation to wheat – from 104,000 acres yielding 23.2 cwt per acre in 1950, to 273,000 acres yielding 57 cwt per acre in 1984/85 – a 646% increase. The barley area has remained fairly static (160,000 acres) but yields have increased from 19.9 cwt per acre in 1950 to 45 cwt per acre by 1984/85, an increase of more than 230%. Sugar beet had only increased by 5% of the 1950 area. The most remarkable transformation has been oilseed rape, from 150 acres in 1970 to over 34,000 by 1985. It is interesting that there are 22,000 acres of woodland on Suffolk farms and only five of the other 56 statistical counties in England and Wales exceed this figure. Suffolk is now one of the leading wine-producers in England, a product virtually unheard of in this area 30 years ago. Apple growing has increased to the point where the county's production is second only to Kent.

Looking to the future it is difficult to believe science can maintain this phenomenal increase. I believe that the plant breeder will produce new varieties requiring less chemical inputs due to greater disease resistance and better quality of grain. Nitrogen fertilisers will continue to be vital. With regard to alternative crops I feel that soya bean varieties capable of growing in Southern Europe could be a significant factor. More home produced protein peas will be used for livestock consumption. One great drawback, particularly to young farmers is that milk and sugar beet are restricted by quota. The most socially acceptable method of 'extensification' is by way of outdoor beef production. Sheep, I think, like cereals and oilseeds are vulnerable to EEC pressures. Pig keeping has closed the cycle of change, and in the next few years I envisage more breeding being concentrated outside, on the poorer free-draining soils. The overheads certainly are much less but the difficulties of extreme weather have to be countered.

Increased computer technology is with us and has already caused some fascinating examples of farming in the future, an example being computer-controlled group housing of sows. This enables large numbers of sows to live in relative harmony being fed by control of a micro-chip in a collar around the neck. The sow will go into the feeding station when she feels like food, and a pre-determined amount will be delivered in front of her.

Inevitably, farmers will have to become more closely involved with the consumer. I believe also that housewives will become bored by the large supermarket chains and will seek fresh, wholesome and more economically priced food by attending 'farmers' markets' and farm shops. It would be wonderful to witness the return of the village shop, selling locally produced and processed food.

Sadly I envisage great pressures on our rural communities. Our government claims credit for low inflation but I cannot imagine house prices are part of the equation. The absurd increase in the price of property, fuelled by high salaries obtained in the city, have made it almost impossible for country people to afford rural housing. With this change comes the 'new villager syndrome' caused by new arrivals from the towns. Suffolk faces a great challenge of change. I would love to believe that our villages will become better places. In the end one has to have faith in Suffolk people whose adaptability, rural commonsense and close proximity to reality will triumph. Indeed in the past, many of those who moved into the county brought with them skills and endeavours that were, ultimately, of great benefit to Suffolk and its inhabitants.

Suffolk farming in 1988 is engulfed by considerable uncertainty, but people will always need food. In 1975 the world population was 4,090 billion, by the year 2000 this will be 6,350 billion – fifty per cent more mouths to feed!

The most dramatic development into the year 2000 AD and beyond will be the use of farm crops for purposes other than as food. Nationally our stocks of energy continue to dwindle – North Sea oil, gas and coal have a limited time span. Despite massive expenditure many are concerned over the safety of nuclear energy. In the long term sugar and grain as replaceable rather than expendable energy stocks may become increasingly vital. Already sugar can be used for a wide range of products such as pharmaceuticals, biodegradeable plastics, disposable nappies and ethanol as a lead free fuel source. If the graph of improved wheat varieties continues as it has done, by 2015 the best crops of wheat could yield 8 tonnes per acre with Suffolk crops averaging 5½ tonnes per acre.

History has shown that agriculture has an uncanny knack of achieving the unexpected. Nobody in the 1950s or 1960s could envisage food surpluses, indeed no-one today can envisage food shortages. Whatever results it is important not just to retain the beauty of Suffolk today but to enhance it, so that future generations will look back on the 1980s and 1990s as a time of real progress.

Norman Scarfe was born at Walton in the county of East Suffolk, went to Felixstowe County Grammar School, and the King's School, Canterbury. He was a Senior King's Scholar; appeared (as Norman Scarge) with Harcourt Williams and Anthony Quayle in *The Zeal of Thy House*, and still hears the jackdaws chuckling round Bell Harry. The love of church architecture began at Lanteglos-by-Fowey when the school moved to Cornwall in 1940. A gunner subaltern in 1943, he joined the battery supporting the 1st Battalion, The Suffolk Regiment, which came ashore through his gun position on a Normandy beach early on D-Day. After that, he kept as far behind the Suffolks as possible. His first book, *Assault Division* (Collins, 1947) recorded his Division's part in the campaign. He was given a copy of Robert Ryece's *Suffolk Breviary* on 1 May, 1945, and so the end of the war signalled the true beginning of his commitment to Suffolk. His recent books are *Suffolk in the Middle Ages* (1986), *The Suffolk Landscape* (revised 1987), *The Suffolk Guide* (4th edn, 1988), *In Praise of Suffolk* (1988), *A Frenchman's Year in Suffolk, 1784* (ed. and transl., 1988), and *Hintlesham Hall: the House and its Associations* (1988). He lives in Woodbridge.

Patterns of Suffolk Building

Norman Scarfe

Drawings by Philip Aitkens

'Preservation can only succeed if it is part of a new creative plan; if the past in fact has a living part in the future.' – Nan Fairbrother, *New Lives, New Landscapes*, 1970.

I like the word 'vernacular', deriving from the Latin for a native 'home-born' slave, *verna*, which is how I often feel; and spreading to mean the local way of speaking and – nowadays – even the local way of building. The trouble is that nowadays there isn't a local way of building. In Suffolk it is being allowed to die out: with us, the avocet has a much better chance of survival. The architects are brain-washed into looking the other way. Only in Essex can a whole new 'Essex' village, Noak Bridge, be seen, wondered at, and cherished. Not the least of its merits is its high density – nineteen dwellings to the acre in its first two phases, higher than almost all new *urban* building in Suffolk. (Later phases are nearer twelve or thirteen to the acre.) For England and

Wales are saddled with the highest density of population in the world: over 800 people to the square mile, even more than in Japan, and compared with a mere fifty in the United States, who scarcely need their skyscrapers; but nor do we. We just need to learn to build densely in the way that, for instance, medieval Nayland is built: now *there*'s a model.

As it happens, the Suffolk tradition starts in the days of the *vernae*, with the walls of the massive fortress of Burgh Castle, raised by the Count of the Saxon Shore to stop the Barbarians entering the Yare and the Waveney at the turn of the third century after Christ. Whether he used slaves, born at home or elsewhere, or soldiers, in the construction of these walls, they are magnificent. They are composed of the local materials: a core of very hard mortared rubble is faced by regular bands of four or five courses of split silver-grey flint, and these bands of flints alternate with bands of red bricks laid in three lacing courses. After lasting seventeen centuries, they are remarkably handsome. A test of good building materials is whether they improve with age, instead of deteriorating. However indirectly or discontinuously, these walls set one of the main patterns of Suffolk building. In their role of keeping out the Barbarians they failed, for here we all are. But after a pause of no more than eight centuries, we began, very, very slowly, to emulate those builders of the late Roman empire.

Walls faced with flint and red bricks: the Romans demonstrate the value and strength of the local building materials and establish a delightful pattern much relished in, for instance, Georgian and modern Beccles.

Indeed, after a mere three and a half centuries, bishop Cedd, the apostle of Essex, was using the materials of another Saxon Shore fortress to build the walls of his nave at Bradwell-juxta-Mare: 24 ft. tall and re-roofed, they still stand to their full height. Here in Burgh Castle, at roughly the same time, the Irish missionary Fursey is believed to have established a successful monastery, but whether some irregular oval patterns in the soil represent St. Fursey's monastic cells is uncertain. The earliest clear dwelling-outlines of our pagan English forebears are to be seen within the bounds of the (later) parish of West Stow. Here, in the earth-holes that once held the vertical main-posts of very small 'halls' and cottages, posts again bear simple rafters and thatch, and the walls are made of vertical tongued-and-grooved planks. This pagan Anglo-Saxon hamlet of two or

Back to rudiments, the plank-walled thatched cottages of earliest Suffolk: West Stow. When did window-openings begin?

three families endured near the river Lark and the Icknield Way for perhaps two centuries before it was abandoned – possibly when the church was built at Stow some distance away. The reconstructed hamlet is truly vernacular, and gives a surprisingly authentic sense of earliest Suffolk. The most universal of house-plans, the simple hall-house, derived from this. A passage, a 'screens passage', divided one end of the primitive hall from the service rooms – pantry, buttery, etc. At the opposite end, where a 'high table' developed, so did a more private apartment for the owner's family. Above this, and within the hall itself, upper rooms came to be added.

The grander Anglo-Saxon halls of Suffolk have so far eluded us. At Yeavering in Northumbria, the royal hall of King Edwin, protégé of King Raedwald of East Anglia, measured 80 ft. × 40 ft. We may guess that traces of a comparable building of Raedwald or one of his immediate successors may one day be uncovered in fairly close relationship to St Gregory's church at Rendlesham. Its magnificence may be imagined from the glittering treasure found at Sutton Hoo, and from what we read of King Hrothgar's hall in *Beowulf*. Wherever these kingly and thegnly Anglo-Saxon and Anglo-Danish halls were, we may be reasonably sure that in essential outline they were wooden aisled halls, like massive barns, with immense oak posts supporting the roofs in the way the stone pillars support the spreading roofs over the aisled naves of our Gothic medieval churches.

For instance, at Cookley, looking across to the woods and coverts of Heveningham (where the one truly grand house left in Suffolk seems curiously precarious), St. Michael's church still reflects the meagre endowment recorded in Domesday Book. It managed to rebuild in stone in later Norman times, with a little square tower and north doorway, but stands partly screened by pine trees. You approach by a five-barred gate and past Church Cottage, which at a glance looks like a semi-detached slate-roofed pair of labourers' cottages. Yet it proves to be a timber aisled rectory of about the time of King John, c.1200, not long after the rebuilding of the church in stone. That the

A wooden aisled rectory at Cookley in King John's day.

rectory was aisled, and the church not, says something about the smallness of that blissful remote parish (as it seems to have been always: no great house, and perhaps twenty to thirty scattered households); and it says something about the convenience, even in modest circumstances, of an aisled structure for a celibate clergyman's accommodation. It also says that patterns of Suffolk building, like the Suffolk character, often lie well below the surface and are hard to read. The best things lie within. Outward appearance is often secondary, however important it now seems in the face of the present huge expansion of numbers.

Only since the 1960s, when Sylvia Colman and David Penrose began here the long business of learning to recognise the age-long evolution of the techniques of the medieval carpenters, have we begun to understand the true

The recent discovery of the great inheritance of aisled halls and detailed medieval house-carpentry in Suffolk.

wealth of our inheritance of medieval houses – the core of our great, unsurpassed, Suffolk treasury of 10,000 Listed

Buildings. Since 1974, the responsibility for their well-being has rested with the councils of the seven newly-created districts, and one has to confess to an overall deep disappointment at their lack of enthusiasm in discharging this duty. Part of the fault certainly lies in our own slowness to appreciate and interpret and publicise the qualities and maintenance-requirements of these extraordinary ancient structures, going back through the eighteenth and seventeenth centuries and right back to the twelfth. Much of the trouble has so far stemmed from the apparent inability, or unwillingness, of the estate agents, members of one of the most affluent trades or professions in our present proliferating society, to rise above the simplicities of advertising their wares as 'Exclusive Period Properties' – whatever that means, it is unlikely to incur penalties under the Trades Descriptions Act.

Roger North (1653–1734), author of *The Lives of the Norths*, was born at Tostock in Suffolk, became a Bencher of the Middle Temple and designed the surviving gateway to it from the Strand. He practised what he preached, repairing his own old house at Rougham in Norfolk, and content merely to add a symmetrical front, with portico, the four columns duly made of flint faced with brick. His delightful writings, *Of Building*, from about 1698, were published by the Clarendon Press in 1981, and described as 'the most entertaining treatise on its subject in the English language'; he asked: 'What more is required of a man than to repair his old house? If there be any faults, as ceilings low, beams seen, or the like, the old house apologiseth' (i.e. its age excuses).

Returning to the surviving, highly articulate medieval patterns I must record that the re-listing of the northern Suffolk parishes has now been carried virtually to completion by Mark Barnard; and with the continuing activities of Sylvia Colman, Philip Aitkens of Rougham, Timothy

Easton of Bedfield, John Bloomfield of Hadleigh and Cecil Hewett and John McCann from Essex, we are now able to understand and enjoy these beautiful buildings, 'hidden' for centuries. Philip Aitkens and Sylvia Colman have described some of them very briefly in the new *Historical Atlas of Suffolk*. Many of them survive only in part. It is in a way fortunate that one of the first of the aisled halls to be detected, and one of the best, should have been in a suburb of Stowmarket already committed to the building of a new housing estate: it was rescued by being dismantled and removed to the Museum of East Anglian Life in Stowmarket, where it can be seen and studied at leisure, though of course out of its own original setting. It stood just within the parish of Combs, and since the nineteenth century was known as Edgar's Farmhouse. In the Suffolk Record Office, I was able to identify the farm as one owned by the Adgor family in 1437. There, in the Ashburnham Papers, and in the Patent Rolls in Chancery Lane, I found John and Ascelina Adgor acquiring farmlands and a house in Combs in 1342 and 1346, and it seems very possible that a rebuilding of this very considerable farmhouse coincided with that new acquisition. The structure had already indicated a building of precisely that prosperous decade. It was clear

Edgar's Farmhouse at the Museum of East Anglian Life: a monument to an enterprising farmer in the 1340s, the decade of the Black Death (1349). Very impressive, yet never a manor house.

from the records that the family was lucky enough to survive the Black Death. What was less lucky, from our point of view, in the 1960s, was that in the rush to qualify for a large grant towards the re-erection of that handsome aisled hall, the builder covered the exterior in a wholly indefensible modern cement-based cladding. It *looks* wrong: worse, it fails to 'live' with the building, develops cracks and the leaks it is supposed to prevent. This is precisely what the Preservation Society and the Museum of

Edgar's Farmhouse – aisled hall

East Anglian Life exist to help Suffolk owners of timber-framed buildings to avoid doing. I go on hoping to see the systematic stripping and re-cladding, in a plaster of slaked lime and sand, of Edgar's Farmhouse as part of the Museum's valuable series of craft demonstrations. I rejoice to see the recent beautiful restoration of plaster and timber in Lavenham's great Guildhall, as I still avert my eye from the fearful stripping away of seventeenth century plaster and historic character from those cottages on the bend of Church Street in 1965.

Before turning to look at external patterns and more general features of Suffolk building, I want us to take in a form probably created and almost exclusively developed in

Edgar's Farmhouse: a reconstruction of its 14th century appearance

Wingfield College: a reconstruction looking towards the service end (east). Raised aisled hall

East Suffolk. It is known as the raised aisled hall, and it is spectacularly demonstrated at Wingfield College. Here, a distinguished aisled (as I think) rectory-house of perhaps Edward I's time was converted into a college of secular chaplains in 1362 by will of the Black Prince's Chief of Staff: the aisle was 'raised' to give more room on the ground floor for the warden and chaplains: their sacrist continued to serve as parish priest. The building now admirably serves as headquarters of the Wingfield Festival of the Arts and Music. An equally magnificent example survives from the Augustinian nunnery at Campsey, and seems to be associated with the creation in 1390 of chambers and common rooms expressly to house canons in an over-optimistic experiment in monastic de-segregation. Here, and in halls

Wingfield College: 18th century facade

at Capel St. Mary, Coddenham, Fressingfield and South Elmham, the ground floor is open – unobstructed by great timber aisle-posts – but aisles are founded upon a massive

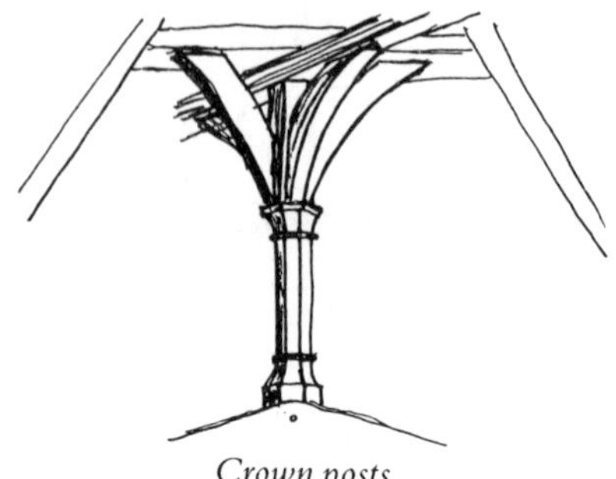

Crown posts

beam just above head height, helping from that level to carry the weight of the notably broad roofs (the only external 'giveaway' of these marvellous hall-houses).

Within the roof space, the normal prop to these medieval

Queen posts

roofs is a single 'crown post', sitting upon the tie-beam (that ties together the tops of the house walls) and preventing, with the aid of a long collar-purlin (see illustration), the

The raised aisle halls of East Suffolk followed by the queen-post trusses: illustrations of the pioneering inventiveness of Suffolk house-carpenters.

collapse of the roof-rafters like a house built with a pack of cards. An interesting development of the 'raised aisle' structure, and therefore an East Suffolk pattern, is the queen-post roof, in which the pair of aisle posts have been abolished from the first floor and banished into the roof.

The much commoner, more familiar, shape among our late-medieval and Tudor houses is the 'jettied' or 'oversailing' first floor. The first reason for employing what at

The explanation of jettying, or oversailing.

first sight might seem a top-heavy structure is, on the contrary, that the cantilever principle is introduced: internal

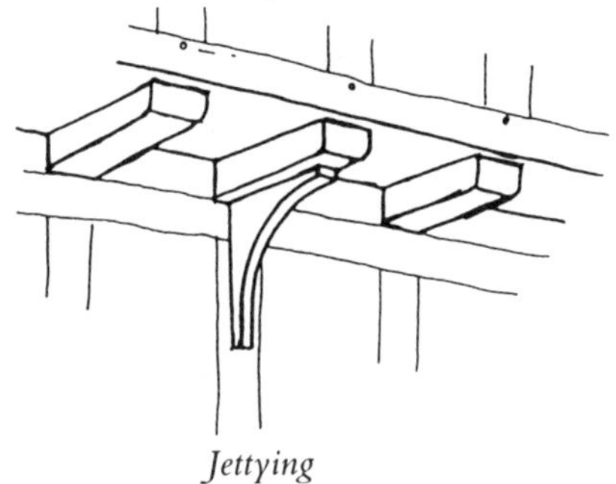

Jettying

and external brackets between ground-floor wall timbers and the projecting floor beams or joists ensure that the slightest tendency to movement by the house frame is corrected by the united pressure of the brackets. A subsidiary reason for the development of jettying is the protection of the lower walls from rain.

Sometimes these jetties, which of course imply two separate storeys divided horizontally by a floor, occur at opposite ends of the frontage of a timber-framed house which, in the middle, has (or had) an open hall from ground floor to roof ridge, the whole house being under one sweep of roof without front gables. Such delightful houses are easily recognised, and are called 'Wealden' houses, from their being more abundant in Kent and Sussex. But one readily thinks of Suffolk examples in Debenham, Hemingstone, Thrandeston, Ixworth and the Bury neighbourhood. Sylvia Colman says that about thirty have so far been counted in Suffolk, mostly late fifteenth-century, but some earlier.

This suggestion of methods imported from the Weald

Wealden House

raises the difficult questions of origins and how one can discern 'Suffolk-ness' in all this: it opens up an enormous subject, big enough for a book on its own.

Suffolk-ness?

Those 'raised aisled' halls, for instance, do appear to be strongly characteristic of East Suffolk. Philip Aitkens thinks this implies the use of local groups of house carpenters, which I suppose is what we would expect. Then there is the crown post, which became fairly general in the later Middle Ages, supporting the roof ridges of houses of almost every class. Aitkens says it seems to have originated in France and to have come first to the southern part of Suffolk, and quite early, c.1300. But the queen posts, because they seem to have developed from the raised aisle idea, can also claim an East Suffolk provenance. Sylvia Colman distinguishes them sharply from the queen posts of other regions, 'where the posts act simply as additional supports below the collar: these we call queen-*strut* roofs in Suffolk'.

We started out with the Romans and their use of flint and red brick to build their fort at Burgh Castle (which was calmly handed to Norfolk in 1974, but which naturally remains in Suffolk for purposes of discussing what occurred during those first 1,974 years). The Roman influence on our building was long delayed. The results of the earliest brick-making in post-Roman Britain are observed in the neighbourhood of Colchester, where such immense quantities of their bricks survived. While they were available in the ruined city, the Roman bricks themselves were re-used. A recent air photograph revealed a splendid Romano-British villa at Lidgate, and for the first time explained the presence of brick in the building of the quoins of the Norman nave of Lidgate church. But at Polstead, within reach of Colchester, the Anglo-Normans *made* bricks for the building of some of the arcades and piers, the clerestory and the chancel windows, showing that they were abreast of the Low Countries and the Baltic in this revival. A century later, it is not surprising to find Little Wenham Hall, in Suffolk and also within reach of Colchester, being built very largely of brick, and furthermore brick of pale yellow with tinges of pink – made from the local gault clay. Built in the 1270s, it is the best preserved of the thirteenth century English houses,

Brick-building. Little Wenham, a landmark in English house-building.

and the earliest known brick house since Roman times. Only four decades later, in the 1310s, very intricate brick vaulting was being built into Butley Priory gatehouse.

Little Wenham has much in common with a house – not of brick, but stone – Moyses Hall in Bury, of a century earlier; also, with a famous illustration in the Bayeux Tapestry of a house a century earlier still: King Harold's manor-house at Bosham, near Chichester. At Bosham (whether or not the 'tapestry' designer has substituted a Norman house-plan for an Anglo-Saxon one, which seems likely), as at Moyses Hall and at Little Wenham Hall, the hall, or main living-room, is clearly on the first floor, above an undercroft, which was presumably the service area and could house armed retainers in times of trouble. Moyses Hall, within the walls and gates of Bury, and fronting the market-place, is designed as a merchant's house, with the merchant living in the traditional way 'over the shop', and is at the same time stone-built, the merchant well able to defend his family and his goods in times of uproar. Behind its enormous moat, Little Wenham's survival in such perfect order presumably owes much to its usefulness as a fortified manor-house in the fifteenth century when its owner was the swashbuckling Gilbert Debenham. It is a tribute to the

The great durability of brickwork: the Suffolk Englishman's home, a brick castle.

sturdiness of brick that in its oldest domestic use in Suffolk it was combined with battlements.

Of course, brick's first widespread use in timber-built Suffolk was in making chimneys to take the smoke from the hall floor up through the roof and clear of the thatch. Builders in Suffolk and Essex often made a great show of these chimneys, and the Howards stuck them round the walls of Framlingham castle to show how cosy the place was! In 1912, Basil Oliver's *Old Houses and Village Buildings in East Anglia* showed these chimneys as triumphs of brickwork already beyond the skill of the craftsmen. By then, Lutyens had learnt to use chimneys boldly, dramatically and with little decoration.

In the Tudor world of Hadleigh Deanery, Hengrave, West Stow Hall, and Christchurch (or Withepole house) near the heart of Ipswich, brick really arrived. At Hengrave, it was the 'white' brick of Woolpit that provides so near a match to such limestone as could be brought. But brick had not wholly taken over from the carpenters and their centuries of timber framing. As you cross the drawbridge at Helmingham, you notice that the front range round the courtyard is timber-framed and brick fronted. An age-long problem with timber-framed outer walls was how to protect the wattle-and-daub filling between the studs (the upright wall-timbers between the main posts). Wattle-and-daub (mud) dissolves in the rain. The usual excellent overcoat was a lime and sand plaster, but when bricks became more available, some owners felt that they would make the best filling between the vertical studs: it was called brick-nogging. The bricks were laid diagonally, or in 'herring-bone' pattern, to help the rain run off. Good examples: Bentley Hall, Dennington Place, Alston Court, Nayland; at Otley, High House and the Hall; at Hawkedon, Swan Hall and Thurston Hall; at Debenham in the High Street; and at Hadleigh, Sun Court is a fine example, rescued by the foundress of the Suffolk Preservation Society whom we remember especially gratefully this year.

As you look at so many familiar scenes, you realise what a luxury brickwork was well into the reign of Elizabeth I. In Debenham street, or at Flemings Hall, Bedingfield, or at Thorpe Morieux Hall, you become aware that brick has been used to dignify the main carpentry structure: an elaborate brick porch has been added. Small pediments in the decoration make a gesture to classical models: the Italian Renaissance has never been taken too seriously by Suffolk builders. At Flemings Hall, the porch is step-gabled for we

The luxury of brick. Brickwork's decorativeness, developed in the Netherlands.

are near the North Sea and feel much more solidarity with the Dutch of William the Silent than with Rome, and do much more trade with them. The stepped gables so familiar here, and the shaped, curved gables, often called 'Dutch gables', seem symbolic of our solidarity, our community of interests. The trellis pattern known as diaper-work (a term that surprises Americans), created by laying bricks burnt to a dark colour as 'headers' (small end of brick to front) to create a diamond pattern, seems to occur as early in Holland as our 'flush' flintwork patterning does here, at Butley: diapering is found in the walls of the ruined castle at Merwede on the edge, now, of Dordrecht, and said to date from the fourteenth century – certainly no later than the fifteenth. It appeared in Suffolk in 1495 in the superb Deanery Towers at Hadleigh and was popular all through the sixteenth century: for instance, in the Willoughbys' house at Parham; in Christchurch, Ipswich and Crows Hall,

Debenham. Through the influence of the great moated Tollemache family house at Helmingham, this form of decorative brickwork was built into a numerous spread of 'Tolly' pubs in this century, and most notably into the former Felix hotel at Felixstowe (now Harvest House).

We have now glanced very briefly at the origins of the main building patterns that give us a sense of 'Suffolk', and we noted Roger North's strong doubt, in the 1690s, whether 'more is required of a man than that he should repair his old house', and at the way he practised what he preached and confined himself to re-fronting his own. This is the first, the leading generalisation about the Suffolk patterns, and the real clue to them: the great majority of our old houses have been merely repaired, given minor improvements, new chimneys and new fronts.

We can see this wherever we look all over old Suffolk, and perhaps most easily in the little towns – Beccles, Hadleigh, Clare, Bungay, Eye, Bury, Woodbridge: it seems to be the characteristic that most distinguishes the treasury of our old houses from the mongrel masses of our new ones.

Let us choose the town of Beccles to examine this assertion in detail. It began as part of the great endowment of

The buildings of Beccles.

Bury abbey. The church's south aisle was completed by the addition of an unusually rich south porch, a beautiful design by any European standards, and originally painted and adorned with sculpture. The English climate quickly spoils external paint on limestone and brickwork (though not on woodwork and old plaster), and both stone and brick actually improve in appearance with the weathering of years. In our climate they are best left unpainted, but in porches and towers there is a case for encouraging the prizewinning sculptors of our art-schools to design suitable figures for these hundreds of blank, accusingly empty, niches. Nobody is likely to accuse of idolatry the artists of this age! We have had three and a half centuries to recover from the austerities that obsessed iconoclastic men like William Dowsing.

Retreating to the secular in Beccles, a building I love as much as any in Suffolk is Leman House, formerly the Sir John Leman School in Ballygate. Seen in the winter sun, its mottled coat – deep-red brick 'headers' set flush with alternate silver split flints – has the rich glow of mosaic, but with the warmth of brick that mosaic lacks. Regular collegiate 'Tudor' windows, some of them going back at least to Leman's foundation in 1631, but the brick and flint front wall is apparently an inspiration of 1762. These are precisely those materials of the Roman Burgh Castle, not far down the Waveney. Near by, in Puddingmoor, Waveney House, now an hotel, has a stunningly beautiful black flint wing with at right angles a dark red brick Georgian façade with giant pilasters. The whole is roofed in dark blue glazed pantiles, a sure sign of Waveney valley building. Here is a serpentine, or ribbon, or crinkle-crankle, wall; they are wavy in plan, and so stand up even if laid only one brick thick; handy for fruit growing; and Suffolk has more of them than any other county, though Norfolk has forty in Yarmouth and Gorleston alone – not far from Beccles. It looks like another 'Suffolk' pattern, though perhaps brought in from the Low Countries through Yarmouth? (It was good to see a length of ribbon wall incorporated in the newly-rescued Angel Yard in Saxmundham recently.)

Still in Beccles, the King's Head hotel faces the Newmarket with handsome regular Georgian red brick features, five bays, three storeys, again giant pilasters. Still in red brick, the hotel curves back along Sheepgate. In front of it, alas, in the market-place itself, are such signs of the impoverished building standards of our age that my pen dries up; and when I think of the remarkable building replaced by

Woolworths in the 1960s, all I can say is: 'With Beccles all round you, how could you!' But as soon as you move out into the surrounding estates, there are acres of this kind of numbness: look, if you can bear to, at the Worlingham Park estate. Yet, exemplary estates, by the architects Tayler and Green, were being built literally on the Beccles boundary, at Forge Grove, in Gillingham, over the years 1955–8 and in the neighbourhood over some twenty years. They could do it, presumably, because they cared about the *genius loci*, the spirit of the place, and because they had the backing of the uniquely sympathetic Rural District Council of Loddon. It

Success and failure in the new estates.

cannot be said that their influence went wholly unnoticed. In Beccles, off the London road, the Cromwell Avenue estate shows something of their stamp: the use of good bricks, and indeed a gable-end with a charming variation on the diaper pattern. But that was back in 1965, since when we have had acre upon acre of Worlingham Park.

The recent debasement of Beccles is repeated in towns and villages all over Suffolk. The beautiful little town of Eye has fared better than most. By 1965, it had developed Bellingham Way quite imaginatively round a large new green. If the council cottages are a shade austere, there is variety, and some pairs have a recessed ground-floor frontage that echoes the vernacular jettying. More recently, the development of the line of the castle bailey with monumental, gabled and chimneyed houses, almost on Lutyens' lines, ranks as one of the most original and admirable additions to Suffolk since World War Two. The warmth of the steep red brick gables is set off by modern roofs of a dark blue material that clearly exclaims 'north Suffolk'. At the same time the angularity of these houses and their grouping round the line of the castle bailey suggests the character of a Norman castle town as surely as if it were in Normandy. That kind of historic sensibility, joined to modern housing needs, is exactly the quality that could redeem the extensions to housing in Suffolk however daunting the scale.

In 1973, the Essex County Planning Department, led by Melville Dunbar, bravely published *A Design Guide for Residential Areas*. Gerald Curtis, chairman of their planning committee, introduced it with these words: 'Few Essex people are happy at the form which post-war housing development in the county has taken. It has a dreary suburban uniformity and lacks any specific Essex characteristics.' The book set out with admirable clarity the policies, the physical and visual criteria, with illustrations in colour of the range of traditional building materials, some horrific pictures of pre-1973 mistakes in Feering, Boreham and Braintree, and details of unacceptable schemes and suggested alternatives.

What could be wrong with this? Critics in Suffolk (and Essex) at once said the 'suggested alternatives' would be

Plea for a Suffolk Design Guide for Residential Areas, *on the Essex model.*

adopted as blueprints by lazy developers, playing safe, and that a new uniformity would spread around the old towns and cottages of Essex. It did, but it was infinitely preferable to the previous 'anywhere' bleakness.

Originally rather sceptical, I lately went to do some checking for myself, pointed in some of the right directions by Tony Aspinall, Mel Dunbar's successor, and John Hunter; and going my own way. I found abundant justification for the *Design Guide*; even in small developments they hadn't listed. The County Council's development of a community of 17½ thousand people at South Woodham Ferrers has much to be said for it, particularly in its new town centre – Chandlers Way and Reeves Way. But South Woodham Ferrers has undoubted imperfections.

The new village of Noak Bridge near Basildon is not

easily faulted – the greatest possible tribute to the principles of the *Guide*, and a lasting memorial to its two devoted, inspired and modest architects, Maurice Naunton and George Garrard. They have created it entirely since 1976, and somehow given it not only the sense of a living village but the sense of an Essex village. I wrote in *Country Life* about its overall qualities. I repeat, the overall density of this new *village* varies between nineteen and twelve dwellings to the acre – a good deal higher than is even attempted in the new *urban* building in Suffolk.

When asked to explain my reservations about our own so-called 'new village' of Martlesham Heath, I have answered, rather uncomfortably, that it is *in*, but not *of*, Suffolk, and could be anywhere. My discomfort derived from the thought that no-one anywhere now seems to be able to capture the feeling of locality in new building. I no longer feel uncomfortable. Naunton and Garrard actually use the words '*genius loci*' that have no meaning at all for the usual products of our late 20th-century architectural seminaries. By *their* words, these internationally-minded professionals reveal their incomprehension, and write of Noak Bridge as 'rustic habitations in Disneyland'. I can only say I rejoice to have lived to see Noak Bridge and meet its modest creators: so do its inhabitants. Whether such a miracle can be repeated, in Essex or in Suffolk, is another matter. Our best, small and wretchedly infrequent successes at present lie in a few extensions to villages, and in infills in towns. One extension, in excellent Tayler and Green manner, looks well as you descend into Bildeston from Needham: Paddocks Way. We look with bated breath as a large development is begun on the hillside immediately opposite. There is now no lack of opportunity for our architects. We can only wish them the dedication and the gifts of Maurice Naunton and George Garrard.

Derek Moore was born just on the border of Suffolk, at Beccles. His interest in wildlife began in infancy when he would bring frogs, newts, voles and any other specimens of interest into the house. After leaving the Sir John Leman Grammar School at Beccles he spent most of his working life with a printer, but continued his interest in natural history in his spare time. In 1985 he turned professional and was appointed Director of the Suffolk Trust for Nature Conservation, now renamed the Suffolk Wildlife Trust. He was the County Bird Recorder for seven years, the Suffolk representative of the British Trust for Ornithology and chairman of the Suffolk Naturalists Society 1982–84. He is involved in a number of other wildlife organizations and is a member of the Research and Survey Committee of the British Trust for Ornithology. He lives in Boxted, Essex, but can see Suffolk clearly from his sitting-room window.

Wildlife on the Heritage Coast

Derek Moore

My first memories of what is now called 'The Heritage Coast' go back to my schooldays at Beccles in the Waveney Valley. Aged twelve my interest in wildlife was already an obsession and I cycled with a friend the nine miles to Blythburgh. My first steps around that beautiful estuary were perhaps the most exciting of my life. This visit on a crisp January day produced my first encounters with shelduck which at that time seemed the most exotic of creatures. Already the males were beginning to chivvy the marginally smaller females into courtship display, and their whistling and laughing calls echoed across the still estuary waters as the bells of Blythburgh church called Sunday morning worshippers. Great flocks of whistling wigeon, packs of precision flying dunlin and the shrill alarm calls of redshank are all memories indelibly fixed in my mind over thirty years on. I remain convinced that my love and enthusiasm for the wildlife of the Suffolk coast began on that wonderful day.

There were other influences of course: one of my school masters was the late G B G Benson of Southwold. He was a teacher in the old-fashioned mould, a disciplinarian but kind and encouraging if you showed some interest. He was a competent ornithologist and at that time the Regional Representative of the British Trust for Ornithology. Whilst I was still at school he invited me on many expeditions to Walberswick, Benacre and Buss Creek, Southwold. The latter was such an exciting place with a muddy lagoon where I learnt to identify many of the similar wader species, and where I first came face to face with spoonbills. Sadly much of the wildlife interest disappeared when the area was drained in the 1960s.

In subsequent years my attention focused on Benacre and Walberswick, both wonderful places particularly for watching birds. The mosaic of different habitats reflected the richness of the Suffolk countryside. How different those days were compared with recent times. Very seldom did you see anybody else with binoculars and if you did you would certainly know them. At this time these sites were not managed as nature reserves and so a good relationship with local gamekeepers was essential. Two such men, Ted Fountain of Benacre and Jack List of Walberswick, are now sadly long passed on but I shall never forget their kindness and their company. As a young man keen to learn all I could about the natural history of the area I benefited much from their knowledge of the birds, animals and insects of the land in their charge. It was in the late 1960s that I first met Herbert Axell, then warden of the RSPB reserve at Minsmere, and this was to radically change my thinking. For the first time I was exposed to a plan to manipulate the land for the benefit of wildlife. Herbert was well into the process of creating 'The Scrape', an area of brackish lagoons and shingle-topped islands adjacent to the sea wall. This was done by using a bulldozer to skim the surface off the grassy sward leaving exposed mud. Islands were shaped, lined with plastic sacks to avoid vegetative growth and then topped with shingle. The results were spectacular and well known. Avocets quickly colonised the area together with many commoner species. At peak migration periods hordes of wading birds stop to feed during their spectacular journeys, and many rarities have been recorded. Soon 'scrapes' were being constructed on nature reserves all over Europe and today much further afield, thanks to the foresight and efforts of Herbert Axell. He has indeed added a new meaning to the word scrape. I now saw the Suffolk coast as not just a place to watch wildlife but as somewhere where, with care and considered management, the natural values could be greatly enhanced. I was by now, I suppose, a conservationist.

The habitats of the Heritage Coast are varied and rich in wildlife. The extensive reedbeds and marshes are the stronghold of many nationally rare bird species. Marsh harriers were reduced to one pair in the country in 1971 when one nest successfully fledged two young at Minsmere. Since then the situation has improved greatly with at least twenty nests in 1988 and as many in the neighbouring county of Norfolk. Avocets have also extended their range since the initial colonisation at Havergate Island and have spread to many other parts of the coast. Bitterns and bearded tits have also maintained their numbers living secret lives in the vast reedbeds. Two mammals have also been of interest in recent years. Firstly the coypu, a large South American rodent which escaped from fur farms just after the Second World War and quickly colonised the wetlands of the Suffolk coast. Its habit of burrowing in the banks of rivers and dykes and of foraging on root crops quickly made it unpopular with man. An eradication programme was set up and it has now largely disappeared from much of the area. Much more exciting has been the recent re-introduction of otters. Despite two animals being killed on roads the project has been successful with young being reared in the wild.

The great estuarine rivers, the surrounding saltmarshes

and freshwater grazing meadows behind the sea walls are an important wildlife resource. The estuarine mud, full of invertebrate animals, and the salt marsh attract many thousands of wading birds and wildfowl both on migration and during the winter. Suffolk estuaries hold internationally important numbers of redshank, ringed plover, grey plover, avocet, black-tailed godwit, shelduck and Brent goose during the winter months. In summer these last areas of East Anglian wilderness are the breeding ground of redshank, ringed plover and oystercatcher.

Our shingle beaches, now much invaded by the ever-increasing flood of visitors, are another valuable asset. The great spit of Orfordness, scarred by the activities of the military past and present, is perhaps the most significant. The flora of these beaches is particularly rich; sea kale and sea pea are just two of the special plants of this valuable habitat and Landguard Point just outside the designated Heritage Coast area is the only known site in Britain for stinking goosefoot. Little terns nest on these beaches as do ringed plovers, both species laying their pebble coloured eggs on the bare shingle. In the last twenty years a large colony of gulls has nested on Orfordness, currently 8,000 pairs of lesser black-backed gulls and 2,000 pairs of herring gulls breed here.

The Suffolk Sandling heaths are one of the great treasures of our coast. The remnants are so valuable that every effort must be made to protect them. Created by man when clearing deciduous forest for grazing, these large tracts of heather and short turf are home to many species scarce in the British Isles. The tiny silver-studded blue butterfly is confined to areas of open disturbed ground latticed with heather and is found on only a few sites. White admirals fly in some Forestry Commission rides where honeysuckle abounds. The open heath no longer echoes to the midnight whistles of stone curlews nor do red-backed shrikes impale their prey 'butcher-like' on the thorns of hedgerows. Stonechats still nest in small numbers and the sweet singing woodlarks have increased their numbers recently as the clear felling of local forestry creates suitable habitat. These clearings interfaced with some trees and heathland also provide ideal conditions for the nightjar. This strange twilight flier arrives every spring from Africa to emit its eerie ventriloquial churring from pine branches. All over Britain this species is declining except, it seems, in East Anglia. A survey on the Suffolk coast showed an increase from 37 pairs in 1984 to nearly 100 pairs in 1987.

The pine forest blocks have been responsible for much of the loss of the valuable heathland but even so do hold some wildlife interest. Crossbills and siskins now nest as do sparrowhawks and the secretive long-eared owl. Birds of prey feature prominently over forest and heathland in the winter; buzzard, rough-legged buzzard, goshawk, hen harrier, red kite and merlin all being recorded with regularity. The pine forest has a remnant population of red squirrels now much decreased and only just holding on. Deer feature also, with red deer numerous in the Dunwich area, muntjac, difficult to see but very widespread, and fallow extremely plentiful particularly in the Tangham and Rendlesham areas. Roe deer have been recorded but remain rare.

There is little significant deciduous woodland within the Heritage Coast area, but just to the west lies Staverton Thicks, an ancient woodland pasture. The oaks contained in this wood are old and gnarled, providing nest sites for barn owls, redstarts and woodpeckers. This is also the best place locally to view hawfinches, large almost tail-less finches which spend most of their life in the canopy and are very difficult to locate. The holly trees in the wood are some of the oldest in Britain, one specimen at over 70 feet is mentioned in the Guinness Book of Records as the tallest in the country. The insect life of Staverton is significant;

purple hairstreaks flit around the tops of oaks and many beetle species found in the rotting timber are special to this site.

These exceptional habitats and their exciting wildlife described above are now subject to accelerating pressures and change. In the last forty years the lifestyle of British people has altered greatly. The motor car has enabled everyone to move around freely and sites often deserted years ago now host thousands of visitors each year. The local population has grown naturally and been enhanced by people moving out, from towns and conurbations, quite prepared to commute to places as far away as London. This has led to more housing development and a more substantial road system. Sizewell 'A' Nuclear Power Station was built in the 1960's with hardly a murmur of opposition and quickly became accepted by local people. How differently was the news of Sizewell 'B' greeted. A pressurised water reactor sowed the seeds of doubt and a three-year-long public enquiry did not stop its construction, which is now taking place. Already Sizewell 'C' is being discussed. Development of dockland at Felixstowe has destroyed parts of the Orwell within an Area of Outstanding Natural Beauty and with the focus on our rivers because of their close proximity to Europe more threats of an industrial and recreational nature must be imminent.

Farming practice in the last forty years has had the greatest impact on our natural habitats. The removal of hedges, trees, grassland and heathland and the introduction of irrigation on to the light sandy soils has enabled farmers to grow good quality root crops. The incentives to develop were substantial and governments apparently gave little consideration to wildlife and landscape features. Now we are faced with surpluses and incentives to take land out of production or to establish practices which return areas to grassland. It seems crazy to the tax-payer and it is a high price to pay for the often permanent loss of so many wonderful places.

I believe the tide is currently turning. Today's farmers are very aware of their responsibilities and encouraged by dialogue with enlightened conservationists are taking steps to restore many features lost in recent years. There have also been natural phenomena which have changed the face of specific parts of the coastline. Severe erosion has occurred in the area from Kessingland sluice to Southwold. The gravel pits at Benacre just north of the Broad have gradually filled up with shingle pushed over the beach, and the former sand dune system to the south has disappeared, allowing salt water into adjacent woodlands. Further south large chunks of the soft cliff fall regularly into the sea, and in the last twenty years at least one hundred yards has been lost, together with a Royal Observer Corps post and a cottage. Some gains have been made with shingle accretion notably at Kessingland and Orfordness.

On October 16th 1987 a hurricane force gale struck East Anglia. Not so much a disaster in my eyes, more of a privilege to see such a dynamic natural happening. The result was that 80% of conifers fell in coastal Forestry Commission plantations which means that there is much new nesting habitat for nightjars and woodlarks, but the future looks uncertain because blanket resowing will end the mosaic of felling and planting which was such perfect management for these birds. With the loss of so many pines one can expect a drastic reduction in species such as goldcrests and coal tits not to mention the rarer crossbill and of course the hard pressed red squirrels. As well as pines, thousands of hardwood trees were lost, particularly around Minsmere. Some replanting will obviously take place but natural regeneration with careful monitoring is my favoured recipe for the future. One great gain from the storm was the great awareness that it created for our countryside in people who had previously given it little thought. Suddenly they realised that great trees were not permanent features.

This leads me nicely to the nature conservation activity which has evolved in and around the Heritage Coast in recent years. Minsmere has been managed as a nature reserve since 1949 and since then National Nature Reserves have been declared at Benacre, Walberswick, Westleton Heath and Orfordness. The RSPB has also set up reserves at Havergate Island and North Warren. The very popular Dunwich Heath and clifftop carpark is owned by the National Trust. The Suffolk Wildlife Trust has grown enormously since its inception in 1962 and its current membership of over 10,000 reflects the growing interest of Suffolk people in their surroundings. Two significant initiatives in recent years should contribute considerably to the protection of two major habitats both in and adjacent to the Heritage Coast area.

Firstly the Sandlings Group was started in 1983 under the guidance of the Suffolk Wildlife Trust and included the Nature Conservancy Council, Royal Society for the Protection of Birds, Suffolk Coastal District Council, Suffolk County Council and the Countryside Commission. This was a unique opportunity to demonstrate how a co-operative effort of several influential but different organisations could effect a common aim. The group set up a project through the Community Programme of the Manpower Services Commission. A project officer was appointed and teams of more than twenty workers began trying to arrest the decline of this beautiful area. Heathland was being lost not only to afforestation, agriculture and development, but naturally from bracken, pine and birch encroachment. The latter was caused by the disappearance of sheep grazing and the demise of the rabbit due to myxomatosis. Much has been achieved but there is still much more to be done. Despite winning the prestigious Ford Conservation Award in 1987 funding is by no means certain to continue to support this valuable work in the future. In 1987 the Trust set up an Estuaries Project with funding from the Central Electricity Generating Board through Worldwide Fund for Nature. This project is initially trying to collate the enormous amount of data already collected on our estuaries and to identify any gaps. Afterwards the project will identify threats to estuaries and to work with interested parties to forestall them. It is important that the project should not only identify dangers and oppose potentially damaging operations through the Suffolk Wildlife Trust but also make suggestions as to how estuarine habitats might be enhanced by practical works, co-operation and discussion. Two significant steps in this direction have already been achieved. Firstly much assistance has been given to local authorities so that they could draw up a management plan for the north shore of the Orwell. Secondly after the Suffolk Ornithologists' Group had successfully campaigned to stop the dumping of rubbish on lagoons at Levington and reached an agreement with the local marina, the Estuaries Project has taken over the task of managing the site and enhancing the area for waders and wildfowl.

There have been many designations placed on sites and areas in the Heritage Coast with a common aim to protect the area and its wildlife. Sites of Special Scientific Interest (SSSIs) abound in the area and the Heritage Coast is itself within an Area of Outstanding Natural Beauty (AONB). In 1971 the International Ramsar Convention was held in Iran to draw up criteria for the protection of wetlands of international importance for which many Suffolk sites qualify, though none of these has so far been officially recognized by the British Government. These sites are also designated as Special Protected Areas (SPAs) under the European

Community Directive on the Conservation of Wild Birds.

With so many designations why should there be such concern? One answer is that considerations called conveniently 'national need' can override SSSIs and AONB areas, while the government can delay formal designations like Ramsar indefinitely for apparently the same reasons.

There is much to be done in the future to highlight the importance of the Heritage Coast for its natural beauty and wildlife, and also its informal recreational potential. There is not necessarily a conflict between the two interests. I firmly believe that the increasing number of people who appreciate and love the area will ensure its survival. You cannot stimulate enthusiasm without showing the public at first hand the richness and variety of habitats and wildlife. This of course must be a planned strategy so that the increased human involvement does not harm the very things we seek to protect. This strategy will only work under the co-operative heading of groups like the Heritage Coast Panel and spin-offs like the Sandlings Group. The Suffolk Wildlife Trust strives to carry out its work in the closest dialogue with all relevant bodies however unlikely the partnership. Close ties have been established with district councils and county councils and their countryside projects, the National Trust, RSPB, National Farmers Union, Farming and Wildlife Advisory Group, Suffolk Preservation Society, Nature Conservancy Council, Countryside Commission and many others. Considerable financial assistance from the latter will allow the Trust through its Reserves Manager to have a significant influence in making controlled access possible for the public to exciting wildlife areas.

The future is a challenge and I believe we can protect that which we cherish most as long as we work together in a practical manner and also unite in strong opposition to those threats which will destroy our natural heritage.

Ronald Blythe was born in West Suffolk and feels that he has 'wintered and summered' the county through most of the changes which it, and indeed all rural Britain, has experienced this past half century, but that he has also experienced its own innate strength to remain itself. Many of his stories and essays reflect the nature of this beautiful, practical, mysterious and occasionally cantankerous place. His books include *The Age of Illusion*, *From the Headlands*, *Akenfield*, *Immediate Possession*, *The View in Winter* and *Divine Landscapes*. He is also a literary critic and has written on Thomas Hardy, Jane Austen, Henry James and Tolstoy. He now lives in the Stour Valley.

Our Villages

Ronald Blythe

Rural life everywhere has both suffered and benefited from the unparalleled changes loosed upon it during the last thirty or so years, and Suffolk's is no exception. Like the rest of the nation in this respect we mourn our losses, and so far have not found a self-convincing language in which to celebrate our gains. Between our sadness for what has vanished, or what is threatened, and our enjoyment of today's comforts, there exists an area of guilt and unease. Words like 'heritage' and 'conservation', until recently part of the vocabulary of small and often abused specialist groups, are now on everybody's lips. So much so indeed that one begins to flinch from their prevalence on the Leisure pages of the press or during any village meeting. As somebody who was born in a profoundly rural West Suffolk and who lived for many years in a remotely rural East Suffolk, and who now stares across the county from a half-lost farmhouse in the Stour Valley (the gale has given me a huge view to Stoke tower), and who has done his fair share of saving this or defending that, I realise that I do have to take some kind of stance on the subject of 'The Village', though what? Should I attempt to reconcile native and newcomer? Should I go over all the old ground as freshly as possible? Should I mug up all the planners' facts and figures for Suffolk's future, the reduction of the corn land and the swelling of the building plots, and alert the village to the possible dangers to come? I would have written on all these things if I thought I was telling anyone anything they didn't know. But after all due consideration, as they say, I decided on a personal – even rather private – approach as the only one which could conceivably interpret the Suffolk village as it approaches the end of yet one more century.

It has to be an indigenous interpretation. Although the argument between native and newcomer is an ancient one which will continue forever, a local writer's or artist's 'voice' is too distinctive for it to pretend to be detached when it comes to describing his own countryside. This does not mean that he decries or laments the non-native. Suffolk, with its long line of little ports facing northern Europe, and its lying in the path of the commerce and culture travelling from London to Norwich, has never known real seclusion. Two of its best village praisers, Adrian Bell and Julian Tennyson, were immigrants, and the writer who more than anyone else saved so much of our old farming practice and language from slipping into oblivion, George Ewart Evans, was Welsh. I grew up in the scenes and history they and others recorded, wholly unaware that anything special was happening, such as an agricultural depression. Looking back, I realise that I had no idea that something tremendous was on the way out and something big enough to take its place was on the way in. What I remember most about the villages was their stillness and poverty, and their rich scents in season of frosty furrows, bluebells, rotting damsons in long grass and chimney smoke, tarring and animals. But my magic book as a boy wasn't by one of the popular inter-war village essayists, it was by Mr. H Munro Cautley, the diocesan surveyer. Published in Ipswich by Norman Adlard and with over 400 wonderful black and white photographs taken by the author, *Suffolk Churches and Their Treasures* stripped away any sense of self-limiting parochialism I may have felt. Many years later, helping to edit Thomas Hardy's novels for the New Wessex Edition, and most of all becoming associated with the John Clare Society, I recognised how early my own symbolic 'reading' of a native landscape had occurred. H Munro Cautley, unlike myself, is fiercely partisan, and I loved him for being so. Because of him the roof over my head was dense with angels. From twelve onwards I walked in and out of what then seemed like an infinity of Suffolk churches, proprietorial and intoxicated. None was ever locked. My bike, a Rudge, began a county wandering and poking about which has never ceased. Each village was both totally like another and completely different.

Such contradictions survive. Neither the intensive farming of the Sixties-on, nor, where some of them are concerned, a doubling of their houses, have succeeded in eradicating their old individuality. It lies just below the surface created by today's romantic and sanitized vision of rural history; the unmistakable face of Stowlangtoft as it showed itself through the ages. Or Rede, the highest village, or the Waldingfields, or strangely eloquent Hoo where, because so little would seem to exist the features remain extraordinarily strong. Debach, the East Suffolk village where I lived for many years, gave this minimal glimpse of itself; yet few places, including brilliant foreign cities, have stamped themselves so uniquely and so uncompromisingly on my mind as this stretch of level fields, World War Two aerodrome and scattering of dwellings. There is nowhere like it.

Except where the Breckland, our lost moor, spread into Norfolk, and along the coast, Suffolk is so thick with villages that its over-all spaciousness, even now, with future population forecasts seeming to threaten in every direction, comes as quite a shock. Once off the motorways or out of the new estates which have been wrapped around most of the old market towns, it becomes apparent that the springing-up of such a large number of Saxon and medieval farming parishes between the Stour and the Waveney has guaranteed lasting solitudes and even, here and there, areas of emptiness. Villages which began in woodland clearings and which still manage to lurk unseen in the dips of an undulating plain until one is almost upon them, retain much seclusion and a lot of uninhabited ground. If you want to comprehend village Suffolk, travel its myriad lanes and tracks, that complex network trodden into the map by the farmers and their stock, by foresters and children, and parsons and lovers, and craftsmen and hunters. If you need to acquire a view which is still outside that of today's tourism, property dealers and regional planners, walk the little roads and river paths. There are thousands of them and they will take you to suddenly unfamiliar villages which you thought you knew quite well.

As well as living in both sides of Suffolk, I have lived on both sides of the second agricultural revolution. The pre-war countryside was ecologically glorious and economically stagnant. Towering hedges were full of the descendants of the oaks which had provided the timber for the houses. Immense elms stood everywhere – coffin wood. The pastures in the river valleys during June rose to the cows' flanks. Cottages were mostly patched, rarely restored, and their gardens unsophisticated and often very beautiful. It was a waiting scene, waiting for a finished Suffolk to depart, waiting for the war, waiting for the post-war transformation. Pastiches of this lost East Anglia are now part of the grist of the tourist industry. It was a world which was still producing its own architectural patterns and colours via local brick and lime kilns, long-strawed wheat and bodging. Many of the larger houses were covered in creeper, ivy, wistaria or Virginia creeper, the latter brought to England by those most celebrated of all Suffolk gardeners, the Tradescants from Walberswick. The house in which Gainsborough's nephew Dupont lived in Sudbury was locked in a wistaria cage.

An extraordinary variety of materials have been used to create the villages and those whose eyes are full of beams and pink, and little else, should take a real look around. Flint, of course, has been both our utilitarian and art stone from the time of the neolithic weapon and tool-makers to the Victorian ploughman who made his garden wall fanciful with the cobs he had turned up. Entire flint cottages were a popular 19th century creation and haven't been much written about. Alec Clifton-Taylor thought that, draughtwise, they were a great advance on lath and plaster. While a lot of the flint came from quarries, much of it was the harsh harvest of the fields. Used merely as rubble filling, as at Bury St. Edmunds Abbey, it could be shocking. However, this is rarely the way the Suffolk traveller will encounter it. Whether set by artists' hands as flushwork on the church exteriors or by farmers into their stockyard walls, whether brilliantly knapped and squared or left in its original weird shapes, flint reflects an aspect of village imagination and practicality which tends to be ignored during the current worship of timber-framing. Stuck among them in some old houses, and certainly in most church towers, you will find sarsens, the ice-borne stones. Village restoration might take into account the intimacy of local materials. That hair holding the old plaster together came from the farm and carriage horses after their groomings, the wall-sticks and tile-pins from the hedges, the clay from the ponds and moats. One small house is likely to contain the work of many generations of local carpenters and odd-jobbers. Sentiment if you like, but better a little of this feeling than to be deadened to the ancient rural consciousness by the ruthless tones of the property market. The swift arrival of popular luxury into a village Suffolk which until so recently was poor and simple, and inhabited chiefly by quiet people with strong views who saw the county as a world, has brought benefit and loss. It is the same everywhere. Unparalleled comfort and guilt and unease. Hence the new vocabulary of the concerned. Not very many years ago, the talk in Suffolk's conservationist groups was that of specialist minorities who must often have felt like King Canute but who now have good reason to feel proud of the stand they took against what then appeared as an ocean of wrong thinking.

Many of these educators came from what might be called the first post-war wave of retired people to settle in Suffolk, and this might be the place to acknowledge their work and achievement. One has only to study the history of the Suffolk Preservation Society itself, not to mention that of every group connected with our ecology, our church, our arts, our industry, our education and our welfare generally, to see that two generations of the retired who have made this county their home have played an enormous role in the ever-continuous business of keeping it safe from the spoilers. The work done here by those who have finished their work is inestimable. The new newcomers are far from retired but because of what the various preservation societies have achieved over the last forty or so years, they are fortunate in entering a village situation which is likely to reveal in every direction evidence of caring and wise thinking. Today's commuting on a county-wide scale is a phenomenon without precedent and must introduce elements into village life which are outside the comprehension of people like myself. It is a late 20th century actuality, and I don't doubt that the old communities which have seen so much will see it through. There is now such an avalanche of printed and filmed matter instructing us all what to do and how to behave in villages that all I will add is, take it gently. Sniff the air before you act. Walk a lot. The cottage garden, the unaffected traditional one, that is, is returning to favour, so consider making it. If you have a shop, pub, forge, chapel, school or even a church, don't let the bureaucrats turn it into a residence called the Old This or That. Never make a mess but don't be obsessively tidy either. Don't garden the churchyard or mow the lane verges when the Queen Anne's Lace has made them magical. Try not to turn all the village past into an entertainment or leisure activity, so as to diminish the the old experience. Don't use a historic church, which is usually a profound work of art, just to arrange flowers in, or hold concerts in, but for its true purpose. Inform yourself on farming, or fishing.

No one as yet knows what effect such coming events as Set Aside, the Farm Woodlands Scheme, Diversification, etc. – all the counter-plans to over-production – will have on Suffolk's villages, but it is bound to be great. Shall we see the old wastes and carrs reappear? Will there be pastures once more and hay meadows? There will certainly be a lot more trees and there will certainly be a rich increase in flowers and insects. Excessive grain growing has altered the character of many villages, destroying their shelter and settings, and there might be now an opportunity to restore what was so drastically taken from them. But I have always loved cornfields and where they have not over-ridden everything before them, I dislike hearing them referred to as 'prairies'. An American friend was intrigued (and a little hurt) to hear the English pejorative use of this word as for him a prairie was a huge stretch of lovely countryside, open and opulent. I walk in the cornfields of the Stour Valley, just as I used to do at table-flat Debach, at every season, seeing them as the *raison d'être* for the existence of all the non-coastal villages, and thus fascinating and powerful. The descent of those to my farmhouse in mid-July is majestic, the ears so dense and crowded, and susurating. King Cunobeline, Shakespeare's Cymbeline, was right to put a wheat-ear on his coinage. Maybe every Suffolk villager, indigenous and new-comer, should visit his local corn in summer and listen to it. It will tell him of the old toil, so unimaginable for us, and of a farm which grew into a settlement, and of a settlement which became a parish, and of work everlasting.

Priority number one in Suffolk's villages for the immediate future is to make it possible for the young descendents of those who built these beautiful places and who worked their farms, made their roads and managed their woods, to stay in them. Unless things change, they will never have enough money to buy houses in them, so they are likely to end up on a town estate. It may be a tough project, but if you see a village as a distinctive and historic group of human beings, and not only as a street of pretty cottages plus a glorious church, then a way will have to be found to conserve its original population. Else it could vanish. Ordinary country people, young and old, are powerless in the face of today's property markets. Our villages are highly articulate these days on every subject and particularly on anything which threatens them. Let their parish councils, PCCs, WIs and county organisations work as hard to prevent young men and women having to leave their home village due to the want of a house as they did to save the landscape. Such fresh exertions, such new targets, won't surprise anyone. It is a Suffolk axiom 'to keep on the goo'. If you don't you die.

Suffolk in Photographs

Julia Hedgecoe

1 Timeless task of spring sowing, here in peat-rich, dyke-dissected allotments on the banks of the River Waveney. In the distance lies Norfolk.

2 Re-roofed and many times repaired, the Smoke House of Lowestoft, built in 1760, continues to smoke and trade in red herrings, bloaters and kippers, whiting, salmon and other delectable tastes.

3 Mr. Robert Claydon, agricultural and motor engineer of Ashley, the village where he was born and where for over forty years he has run his business. Mr. Claydon's smithy extends into a more up-to-date garage where his skills with motor vehicles are sought from great distances and by owners of valued veteran vehicles.

4 Kate and Peter Campbell's bedroom at Eye Priory. The ceiling beams suggest the original priory from which the present house was built after the Dissolution.

5 Meadows of apple blossom fringe Debenham each spring producing their harvest for Aspalls' cider factory. Established in 1728, today's output of apple juice and cider vinegar has overtaken the now smaller demand of 260 years of cider making – and drinking!

6 Richard Clay of Bungay, printers and binders of books

established 112 years. The family line has continued, the printing works grown to possibly the largest book producers in Europe with 100 million hard and paper-back books leaving the Bungay works each year.

7 Pigs have moved out into the fields again – thanks to EEC price restrictions indoor housing has become too expensive. This happy sow has her own det. res. above Stowlangtoft.

8 Roots and branches encase the centuries-old hill climb from pretty Dalham village ascending to Hall and Church.

9 Working outside on a summer afternoon at Wenhaston Primary School where Mr. Marshall has forty-four pupils. For ever may it survive!

10 From the Abbey Gate, Bury St. Edmunds, two ladies enjoy a seated view of the botanic gardens established in 1850. Far-sighted Alderman Clark and Alderman Nice had these gardens opened to the public in 1912, since when hundreds of thousands of people each year enjoy the space and the flowering alongside the Abbey ruins.

11 High on a ridge above the River Stour stands the recognisable silhouette of Stoke-by-Nayland's church tower. Were there continuous summer mists when Constable enjoyed this same scene or is air pollution the cause?

12 Crag Path, Aldeburgh, its narrow height creating both intimacy and solid protection from the sea which these houses serenely face on the other side.

13 Miss Smith in the Post Office where she was born and where she has worked since her mother was seventy and 'needed a hand'. Her memory is long; as a child she recalls the postman arriving early on his bicycle loaded with parcels on the front carrier, a satchel full of letters

Captions continued on page 113.

BUILT 1780
RAINBOW TROUT
LONGSHORE HERRING 60p
FRESH BOILED CROMER CRABS FROM 50p READY NOW

SUPER

5

6

7

8

9

10

11

12

13

14

15

16

17

18

19

20

DID IT FOR

on his back, often with the words 'blasted head-wind to get here this morning.' Her mother would do the sorting on the same counter that stands today, her father then setting off to do the morning deliveries, Christmas day included.

14 Lovely Suffolk estuaries where green fields offer security to sea-going boats. The River Deben at Woodbridge.

15 Ipswich Customs House first graced the dockside in 1843, much later to be dwarfed by the malt warehouse on one side and now amusingly reflected in the new Contship building, a shipping agent, on the other.

16 Where the beach meets Felixstowe's expanding docks, sunbathers and fishermen, cargo ships and north sea ferries share the River Orwell's seaside.

17 Huge bales of straw look like a giant's game of draughts set out beneath a stormy sky at Wordwell.

18 Small fields and soft, hilly landscape rising from the Stour valley near Higham.

19 Cherished timber frames of Lavenham, looking down Lady Street to the Priory.

20 The Butterfly has weathered three centuries alone among fields set a good mile from Great Finborough, its earliest timbers suggest two more centuries as a smaller dwelling.

21 Porch carving on Brook House, Long Melford.

22 Flint flushwork is to be found all over Suffolk on large and small churches alike; this beautiful example is at Fressingfield.

23 Newly repaired and freshly polished, beautiful Denston church. Fifteenth century carved bench ends set against eighteenth century box pews.

24 Visitors enjoying The Nutshell at Bury St. Edmunds, reputed to be the smallest pub in England.

Peter Underwood was born in London of Suffolk parents. His family's roots go well back into the county's past. He came to Ipswich as a child in 1933 and has remained there ever since except for war service in the RAF and a period at Oxford. He is a geographer by training, but is an architect manqué and was a schoolmaster for 32 years.

He was a founder member of the Ipswich Society, was the chairman for 14 years and is now vice-president.

He has also been chairman of the Eastern Federation of Amenity Societies and of the Ipswich Conservation Advisory Panel since it was formed.

A long-standing advocate of Home Rule for East Anglia, he lives in a mid-Victorian house ten minutes walk from the centre of Ipswich.

A Tale of Two Towns

Peter Underwood

'They say that in the unchanging place,
Where all we loved is always dear,
We meet our mornings face to face,
And find at last our twentieth year.'
Hilaire Belloc

A sense of place is something we all have when it applies to locations associated with memorable experiences. For most of us there are scenes to be recalled from childhood, and our judgement of places is coloured by the degrees of pleasure we experienced there. But what of our more everyday perceptions of place? It has been said many times that we are a rural people at heart, and it is undoubtedly true that a ready response to 'country' and 'natural' things is widespread. It is only necessary to consider the images used by advertisers to have this confirmed. In a generalized way perceptions of place are that rural is 'good' and urban 'bad'. Furthermore, the more 'unspoilt' the countryside the better it is, whilst the more 'developed' the town the worse it is thought to be. I suspect that many of my readers prefer the country to the town, and when it comes to towns I hear them pointing out that some towns are better than others.

What then of our two county towns? Or more correctly,

what of our county town and its erstwhile companion in that role? I think I have it right: the accepted judgement is that Bury St. Edmunds is a town of better quality than Ipswich. Certainly it has more mentions in the tourist literature, although the obvious reason for that is the tangible presence of the abbey, no historical dimension of a comparable nature being possessed by Ipswich. There is no doubt that towns with substantial medieval structures, such as castles, cathedrals, abbeys, walls and gateways readily attract visitors because the average person can easily comprehend their antiquity, even when in a ruinous form. Had the Ipswich castle survived beyond the year 1176 perhaps the town would have been regarded by popular opinion as a historic place, and traditionally accepted as a town to be visited.

Virtually all the descriptive books about Suffolk published earlier this century had less to say about Ipswich than about Bury St. Edmunds, but since the mid-1970s this has been reversed. The same applies to historical works, for historians have changed their attitudes towards Ipswich, acknowledging that it has a past worthy of more detailed comment. It is clear that both scholars and commentators, as well as interested members of the public, have come to know more about Ipswich in recent years. The last decade or so has seen a significant change, and not just because the town has made itself more attractive to visitors. Archaeological investigations conducted by Keith Wade and Tom Loader have dramatically demonstrated the importance of the origins of Ipswich.

We must bear in mind that historians rely on words – place names and documents – but archaeologists have artefacts and organic remains on which to establish their ideas of our past.

The Venerable Bede wrote about the Wuffingas, the ruling family who had established unity throughout East

Anglia by the middle of the sixth century. Raedwald who was King from 599 to about 625 was the most distinguished of them, being acknowledged as Bretwalda or overlord of all the other Anglo-Saxon rulers. No document records that it was he who was buried with magnificent treasures in a ship at Sutton Hoo, but the archaeological evidence is very strong. Bede tells us that King Raedwald had a palace some four miles away at Rendlesham but so far there is no archaeological support for this. However we do have abundant archaeological evidence now, that Gipeswic (Ipswich) was a significant port and manufacturing town dating from that time, and it is quite probable that Raedwald was involved with its origins. His successor King Sigeberht founded a monastery at Bedericesworth (Bury St. Edmunds) and, according to Bede, retired to live there in about the year 630.

It seems reasonable to give equal credence to archaeologists and historians, perceiving both Bury and Ipswich to have had royal connections in the early seventh century, the one as a small centre of Christianity and the other as a maritime trading and industrial town.

Both towns are historically important because their medieval street patterns have survived. The distinctive grid of streets at Bury dates from the expansion of the town immediately after the Norman Conquest, and represents an early example of English medieval town planning.

There have been assumptions that the precise rectilinear layout of Roman towns was the inspiration for all such planning in later centuries. This certainly need not have been so since it is a reasonable design for anyone to use when laying out a town, especially if precision is not a prime intention. Indeed it may well have been the original form adopted for the expansion of Ipswich which took place from about AD 750. Parallel north-south cobbled streets, one of them being an original alignment of St. Stephens

Lane, have recently been discovered at the archaeological site south of the Buttermarket, a street which itself is almost certainly one of the east-west alignments. If this is confirmed by further archaeological investigations we can regard Ipswich as one of our earliest post-Roman urban developments, and perhaps the first English planned town. What makes it even more important is that it is the only one out of a handful of Saxon trading ports around the southern North Sea which has had an unbroken history of occupation on its original site. Ipswich was founded as a port to trade with the Rhineland and it is still doing so fourteen centuries later.

The martyrdom of King Edmund in 869 eventually led to Bury becoming a major place of medieval pilgrimage, and even after that it continued to be visited by the crowned and uncrowned alike. As a centre of commercial wealth easily reached up the tidal Orwell, Ipswich was attacked by the Danes and devastated in 991 and 1010, but seems to have recovered by the Norman Conquest fifty years later. However Domesday Book reveals that during the twenty years up to 1086 in Ipswich 'there have been laid waste 328 dwellings', whereas Bury had gained 342 on what had been 'St. Edmund's arable'. Historians infer that this was because Ipswich was sacked by William I during his suppression of the rebellious Earl Ralf Guader (Wader) sometime after 1076. Archaeologists have recently found evidence of defensive works, battlefield burials and burnt buildings which appear to confirm these Ipswich misfortunes. Norman Scarfe has concluded, 'Ipswich had tremendous natural advantages, its harbour, and its healthy abundance of fresh water, and doubtless soon recovered its strength'.

Is this the right picture of our two towns? Did both have royal favour in the early years of the English nation, but was it Bury which enjoyed a continuing superior status while Ipswich had to make its way through economic adversities by its own resources? It is certainly intriguing to ask if each is still essentially what it was in early centuries. Is Bury still a town for visitors, many of them still buying their souvenirs of St. Edmund, as the medieval pilgrims did, and a centre for county families who still expect a better class of service? Is Ipswich a workaday town concerned primarily with trade and commercial services, where tourists still do not find anything to interest them?

Without doubt there is a core of truth here, giving us a fascinating glimpse of unchanging habits. Nevertheless I suggest that such a limited concept does not lead to fruitful appreciation, and we must explore some aspects of both past and present for a better understanding of Ipswich and Bury St. Edmunds.

It has been pointed out that Bury has 'always had visitors', and that active promotion of what we would now call tourism took place there during the eighteenth century. For six centuries pilgrims travelled to the shrine of St. Edmund's Bury, but that sort of visiting came to an end with the destruction of the abbey church in 1539. Ipswich also lost an important shrine at the Reformation. The Chapel of Our Lady of Grace, just outside the West Gate in Lady Lane, lost its miraculous statue of the Virgin in 1535. This had been visited by monarchs and many persons of eminence over a period of some four centuries, and was said to rival Walsingham as a place of pilgrimage. However there does not appear to have been any effort on the part of the gentry and merchants of Ipswich to encourage tourists, that is visitors for health and recreation reasons, some two hundred years later.

Indeed it was during early Georgian times that the towns diverged in character, Bury becoming a social centre for 'the quality' whilst Ipswich diversified its port and market functions, both towns suffering from a steady decline in the cloth trade. Defoe was aware of this in 1722, describing the potential he saw for the port of Ipswich and then remarking: 'There is a great deal of very good company in this town, and though there are not so many of the gentry here as at Bury, yet there are more here than in any other town in the county, and I observed particularly that the company you meet with here are generally persons well informed of the world and who have something very solid and entertaining in their society'. He reports of Bury, 'It is crowded with nobility and gentry of all sorts of the most agreeable company', and, 'Here is no manufacturing in this town, or but very little, except spinning, the chief trade of the place depending upon the gentry who live there, or near it, and who cannot fail to cause trade enough by the expenses of their families and equipages among the people of a county town'.

There is a lack of Georgian elegance in Ipswich when compared with Bury, and a superficial judgement is often made that it is because Ipswich was not sufficiently prosperous during the eighteenth century. I believe it is easy to be misled into thinking that this difference between the towns is to be explained solely by economics. During the last twenty-five years or so it has become increasingly realised that there was a great deal of 'inverted facade -ism' going on in Suffolk during the eighteenth-century. Timber-framed buildings were not only having their windows changed to a double hung sash style, but many were also having their frontages completely rebuilt in either the local warm red or stone-cool white bricks. What appears to be of the eighteenth or early nineteenth century from the front is really Stuart, Tudor or even earlier behind. Certainly there were some completely new town houses built, in Ipswich as well as Bury, but most of what appear to be gentlemanly Georgian were older houses refronted, and towards the end of the century, as business improved, many more received this treatment.

By the time Victoria succeeded to the throne there were Georgian and Regency frontages along the north side of Tavern Street in Ipswich, the result of a remarkable street widening scheme in 1815–18, and in several stretches of Northgate and Upper and Lower Brook Streets, with more isolated examples in other parts of the main town. The first ten years of the Queen's reign saw building in a similar style along the newly created Museum Street, Arcade Street and Colman Street, all on garden land within the old town. Outside the historic area the first sections of High Street, Berners Street and Fonnereau Road, together with stretches along the roads towards Norwich and Woodbridge, had also appeared in the Regency manner. Many of them, like those in Bury, were provided with splendid doorcases with classical features which can still be admired.

When the railway reached Ipswich and Bury in 1846–7 both towns must have had a similar architectural appearance. Ipswich then had twice the population of Bury so its features were not so compact, but there was a substantial Georgian elegance set against a background of painted plaster on jettied timber-framed buildings, up-dated with sash windows, with steeply pitched roofs of clay tiles. Each town also had some larger buildings, roofed in slate at a low pitch, and with parapets, pediments, pillars and porticoes in the Neo-Classical style.

In Ipswich such buildings were; the Royal Cavalry Barracks (1795), Theatre Royal (1803), Corn Exchange (1810), Town Hall (1818), New Assembly Rooms (1821), Hospital (1836), Temperance Hall (1840), Custom House (1844) and Museum (1847). In Bury there were the Town Hall or Market Cross (1780), Athenaeum (1789), 82 Guildhall Street (1789), Theatre Royal (1819), Corn Exchange (1837) and St. Edmund's R C Church (1837). Each town had its hotel which would gain fame from its Pickwickian association, the Great White Horse being Regency and the Angel

Georgian, but both having striking individual doorways.

I suggest that when the young Charles Dickens first visited the two Suffolk towns in 1835 and 1836 their architectural characteristics would have struck him as much the same. Ipswich would have had a greater proportion of buildings of the fifteenth to seventeenth centuries, and there would have been noticeable differences in that the streets of Bury were wider and straighter. Although Ipswich was obviously bigger, from the central streets of both towns he would have been able to look out towards wooded farm and park lands. There would also have been a pleasing visual contrast between the narrowness of busy streets and a wider vista in each case. Bury had spacious Angel Hill, where the great medieval fairs had been held, and the abbey grounds stretching to the river meadows and the old vine grounds beyond. Ipswich had the maritime scale of the quays and the tidal sweep of the River Orwell to provide a comparably important foil.

I am sure that to our eyes they would both have been very attractive towns, as they were to William Cobbett visiting in 1830. 'I proceeded to Ipswich, not imagining it to be the fine populous and beautiful place that I found it to be . . . Ipswich is in a dell, meadows running up above it, and a beautiful arm of the sea below it. The town itself is substantially built, well paved, everything good and solid, and no wretched dwellings to be seen on its outskirts.' When he came to Bury he said that not to sing its praise 'would offend every creature of Suffolk birth: even at Ipswich, when I was praising that place, the very people of that town asked me if I did not think Bury St. Edmunds the nicest town in the world . . . and indeed, as a town in itself, it is the neatest place that ever was seen. It is airy, it has several fine open places in it . . . '. The question must be asked: why was Ipswich so much less regarded as a social centre a century later?

In finding the answer we must first acknowledge that by the early years of the nineteenth century Bury St. Edmunds was generally accepted as a town of quality. A hundred years earlier the second Earl of Oxford had published an account of the place which was not by any means all praise, but did establish that it was somewhere worthy of aristocratic attentions. This was the crux of it, the higher levels of society demonstrated by their presence throughout the eighteenth century that Bury was a town to be highly regarded, and the lower orders followed them in that belief.

What turned out to have been a major point of change for Ipswich took place during the first five years of Queen Victoria's reign. In 1837 Henry Palmer produced his engineering plans and designs for the Wet Dock, its quays and warehouses. In 1842 the opening ceremony was held for what was then the largest enclosed dock in the country, and the twelve-hundred-years old port immediately moved into a new age of growth in trade and industrial development. The town's new status was confirmed in the year of the Great Exhibition, 1851, when Albert, Prince Consort, visited the meeting of the British Association for the Advancement of Science then being held in Ipswich.

Victorian enterprise expanded and diversified the manufacturing, processing, constructional and distributive activities in the town, and retailing, clerical and domestic servicing developed in parallel. The growing labour force was housed in and near the historic centre. Yards, gardens and backlands were built on, creating cramped and crowded courts. Land immediately outside the line of the Saxon and medieval defensive ditches was covered with small terraced houses. Rebuilding in the commercial and professional parts of the town took place in a piecemeal way. Town houses became shops, and the more successful shopkeepers and professional men soon built substantial houses and imposing villas on areas of rising land along roads leading out of the town, and in the intervening spaces.

In the traditional shopping and business areas of Ipswich premises were rebuilt more than once in several instances, often in association with street widening, but never to an overall plan, not even when associated with the creation of Princes Street, a new route from Cornhill to the newly built railway station (1860). Such architecture tended to be increasingly imposing in scale, but usually managed to lose the tradition of Regency balance and proportion in the process. Fortunately the work of such local architects as E F Bisshopp, J S Corder, T W Cotman and H J Wright produced some late Victorian and Edwardian buildings of distinction. The public buildings around the Cornhill – Town Hall, Post Office and Corn Exchange – were rebuilt as we see them today, and four banking companies commissioned buildings of character which contribute to this scene of Victorian administrative and commercial confidence.

What then was the situation at the outbreak of World War I: how did Ipswich and Bury compare?

During the seventy years from the first decade of Queen Victoria's reign to the accession of King George V Ipswich had increased its population by 191%, compared with a rise of only 34% for Bury. Ipswich had gone from twice, to four and a half times the size of Bury. Obviously there was much more rebuilding and expansion at the one than at the other. In fact the eastern suburbs of Ipswich, known as California and Rosehill, had grown to cover an area equal to the whole of Bury, and they had their own railway station at Derby Road.

Until about 1875 new housing in Bury consisted mainly of infill developments in the historic town, including Brackland, and it was only in the second half of the period that the Victorian and Edwardian suburbs, which now constitute the Conservation Area to the west of the ring road, were developed.

So, whilst Ipswich became a markedly Victorian town, with a mixture of historical survivals and new buildings in the town centre, surrounded by new suburbs, Bury changed much less, and retained its Georgian ambience.

Between the wars Ipswich and Bury became even more differentiated. An extensive programme of slum clearance was carried out in Ipswich. The cramped and neglected courts attached to old timber framed houses, and the rows of small terraced houses in which several generations of industrial and domestic workers had grown up, were cleared away, particularly from the notorious areas known as the Mount and Rope Walk. New council estates appeared towards the north-west and, particularly, the south-east boundaries of the borough.

Throughout this period the population of Ipswich went from four and a half times to five and a half times that of Bury, whose growth was only 7% compared with 35% for Ipswich. There were some changes in Bury, the greatest of which was the coming of the sugar beet factory in 1925, but new building there had nothing like the impact it did in Ipswich, where civic pride in anything other than commercial gain seems to have been steadily eroded. There *were* protests at the loss of fine old buildings which had survived the Victorian and Edwardian redevelopments, but these were mainly by individuals, many of whom were in the forefront of the foundation of the Suffolk Preservation Society.

I first became aware of the significance of it all as a schoolboy in 1937, when I watched the demolition of the timber-framed Waggon and Horses Inn, next to the Ancient House in the Buttermarket, to make way for the latest in cinema design. The Ritz (or ABC) has just been pulled down in its turn. It is sadly ironic that one has to say that fifty years was about what it deserved compared to the ten times older structure it replaced. A frequently heard comment of the day was, 'Ah, but you can't stop progress you know'.

What was the attitude in Bury St. Edmunds? I have to submit that the evidence suggests it was the same as in Ipswich. Indeed, leaders of the worthy community of burghers in each town persisted in their philistine attitudes towards architecture and townscape until well into the second half of the twentieth century, as we shall see.

The ten years following the end of World War II in 1945 was a period of new thinking. A series of Town and Country Planning Acts gave local authorities the power to replan, and to list buildings of historic and architectural interest. The Ipswich Town Plan appeared in 1954 showing an inner ring road carving through the historic core. Fortunately events overtook construction, and we only have part of it: Civic Drive. Recently Cromwell Square has been created – perhaps as a reminder of where it stopped!

Redevelopment on a big scale was the order of the day in the centres of many of our historic towns, and in Ipswich there was a competition for local architects to redesign the Cornhill, including the site of the Town Hall and Corn Exchange! Valuable historic buildings were still being lost. Felaw's House in the upper part of Foundation Street, the part Tudor part medieval house of a benefactor of the grammar school, and the Half Moon public house, with its famous fox and geese corner post, at the southern end of the same street, were two notably disastrous examples.

In 1960 the Ipswich Society was founded, at about the time that two 'comprehensive redevelopments' were being designed. These were to prove to be horror stories, both architecturally and economically. The more infamous was Greyfriars, now being rescued and imaginatively recreated under the ownership of Willis, Faber and Dumas Limited, who put this part of Ipswich on the world's architectural map when they commissioned Norman Foster to design a new headquarters for them. The second town centre redevelopment of the early 1960's was Carr Precinct, and that is still with us unfortunately. I find it particularly awful in its grossly insensitive scale and coarsely conceived composition. I think its fabric is at least as bad as Greyfriars ever was, and it would be a delight to hear that it is suffering from one of those fashionable concrete diseases.

Between 1964 and 1969 Ipswich was being considered for a major expansion scheme, and planning and investment were retarded. In retrospect this was not a bad thing as it gave time for the townspeople to learn from what had been going on elsewhere. Their elected representatives also began to understand what the Ipswich Society and others had been saying. A new planning department was set up, and up to date surveys and reports were put before the council. By the time local government reorganisation had taken place in 1973 an important corner was being turned in Ipswich affairs.

In the mid-1970s the first Conservation Area was designated and an advisory panel set up. A building preservation trust and historic churches trust both came into being, the latter specifically to look after the redundant churches. The Ipswich Society began its survey for a Local List in 1977 and published it in 1984, with full photographic and descriptive details of some six hundred buildings. Meanwhile the Statutory List was being updated. The District Plan for the Central Area was begun in 1978, and in force three years later. One of its major proposals was for the paving of the main shopping streets so that pedestrians could have priority, and this work will be done by the end of 1988.

In Bury during this period something similar had been happening, but in the main several years later than in Ipswich. During the 1960s West Suffolk began to take overspill population from Greater London, and it was envisaged that the population of Bury would reach 40,000 by the early 1980s. In the event it is about 10,000 short of this number, but it has been growing faster than Ipswich during the last ten years, and is now back to a quarter of the county town's population.

Like Ipswich, Bury has post-war housing estates of very mixed quality, which now extend to the borough boundaries. The Bury Town Map of 1962 and its revisions indicated areas for this expansion, including Moreton Hall land, and also suggested substantial central area redevelopments for Cornhill which would have demolished the Corn Exchange and Public Library. Getting these errors of judgement corrected took considerable effort by the Suffolk Preservation Society and its supporters. During the process the Bury Society was formed in 1971 and together, by demonstrative and constructive argument, they managed to save views across to wooded farmland at Moreton Hall, and to keep the architecture of the historic market place reasonably intact. Bury now has two Conservation Areas, with an advisory committee since 1984, and the current Local Plan indicates appropriate policies, which must be followed if Bury is to keep its pleasing character.

What then is the situation in our two towns? How should they be changing towards the end of the century?

Although different in character and size both towns are under pressure from people and vehicles, not so much when moving about as when they are at rest. The by-passes and other road provisions have been controversial but they have taken through-traffic away from central areas, which is where car parking demands are increasing, and where meeting them will be difficult and expensive. Multi-level parking will surely come to Bury, and if it were to get cars off Angel Hill it would be a blessing. When more permanent car parks with effective accommodation sign-posting are provided in Ipswich drivers may be able to find them, and so use them more efficiently.

Neither Ipswich nor Bury has yet got a pleasant, safe and efficient station for buses on out of town routes. Obviously it is in the interests of everyone to get this resolved soon. Shoppers who come in by bus presumably will not be using the out of town superstores, but will be attracted to the new shopping arcades, malls and centres, where they will find the interiors quite dramatic and exotic. This may not make up for a limited choice of goods, however, and unless small specialist shops and those offering genuine quality are to be found there, customers may not take to the new shopping experience in sufficient numbers. Competing outlets for fad clothes, shoes and jewellery, disc music and video entertainment, represent a small range of offerings on which to build the new consumer opportunities. Each town has an example and there are more to come, so we must hope that wider competition will bring commercial success for all!

Ipswich in particular will have its historic centre massively influenced by the exterior architecture of these new shopping developments, and there have been anxieties over the appropriateness of their designs. The human scale, which mercifully is still very apparent in the heart of even our largest Suffolk town, has to be matched. Considerable architectural skill is required to achieve this when the area being redeveloped is relatively large. It must not be attempted by the addition of 'traditional features' but by using materials and forms in sympathetic proportions. Everything possible must be done to push the entrepreneurs and their designers towards this.

The Secretary of State for the Environment has just rejected schemes for large housing developments in attractive countryside at Westerfield and Chantry Vale on the outskirts of Ipswich, with a six months conditional delay on a decision about Belstead Brook, where road problems must be resolved. This is good news since much more consideration must be given to how our towns relate to the rural areas around them.

Developers of housing land prefer a large flat open space, and design their layouts accordingly. At both Bury and Ipswich there are housing estates where awkward retaining walls, absurdly steep access drives, and windows looking towards adjacent walls rather than across to open views, demonstrate a lack of imagination which is inexcusable where sites have attractive slopes.

St. Edmundsbury Borough Council must resolve the problem of thirty year's neglect and disagreement over the Abbey West Front. This requires active co-operation with Bury Town Trust, the Bury Society, English Heritage and all others who have a role to play. After all, what they have is an Ancient Monument of outstanding importance.

Ipswich Borough Council must ensure that developments around the Wet Dock take place according to an agreed plan rather than by piecemeal catchpenny opportunism. The potential for this exciting townscape of quayside industries, converted warehouses and new sites for a mixture of commercial, housing, leisure and cultural uses has already been acknowledged. A conference is being held so that interested parties may contribute, and this will involve the Ipswich Port Authority, industrialists, developers, environmentalists and statutory authorities. It is vital for the future quality of Ipswich as a town that such co-operation is successful. After all, those who planned the Wet Dock one hundred and fifty years ago showed the way by providing a striking Customs House and a tree-lined promenade beside the New Cut.

Bury is still a very attractive town to walk round, and with more streets freed from motor traffic it will be even better. Ipswich is much improved since those days when parked vehicles, trolley bus poles and wires, and large advertisements cluttered the scene. Both towns have deservedly been winners in the Britain in Bloom competitions, and Ipswich is particularly fortunate in its parks and leisure facilities. If the Ipswich Archaeological Trust succeeds in getting a 'Gipeswic Centre' which will excite visitors by informing them of the town's unique story about its Saxon origins, and if developments beside the Wet Dock are such that we have the European Visual Arts Centre there as another attraction to a wide range of visitors, there will be gains for the whole of Suffolk.

John Clayton was born in London. He was Chief Executive of the Ipswich-based Pauls Group of Companies (then Pauls and Whites Plc) from 1970–82 and was chairman of the Eastern Region Council of CBI 1974–76. He is a Suffolk County Councillor, chairman of the Agricultural Training Board for Great Britain and a director of several companies. He was founder chairman of the Ipswich Enterprise Agency and was, until recently, chairman of the Ipswich Historic Churches Trust. He was awarded the CBE in 1987 for services to industry and agriculture. He lives in Hadleigh.

Trade and Industry – A Personal View

John Clayton

Since earliest times trade and industry have played a significant part in forming the Suffolk we know today. Sometimes in support of the county's agricultural base, sometimes because of our proximity to the Low Countries and sometimes in response to the demands or difficulties of London's growth.

As long ago as 3000 BC axes were being imported from Cornwall and the Lake District for Suffolk's first farmers until our own flint deposits near Brandon were discovered and exploited. This may well be the longest surviving industry of all time, for in the Napoleonic war Brandon flints were still said to be the best in the world for firearms and as recently as 1846 a limited company was formed to carry on the industry. But the development of the percussion cap put an end to it and the people of Brandon turned to rabbits, supplying skins to glue manufacturers and preparing the fur for hatters.

Suffolk's international trade was established by the Bronze Age and there is evidence of contact with Iceland, Northern France and the Low Countries since 2000 BC.

Bronze and gold and wine were certainly being imported for several hundred years before the Roman invasion and migrations of craftsmen were improving local technology.

Other than flint, the first recognisable manufacturing industries seem to have been developed in Roman times. Pottery was made on a large commercial scale at West Stow and Wattisfield for example. Salt was being produced by evaporation in the estuaries, wool production was well-developed. These, with other agricultural produce and slaves, provided the exports to pay for the rapidly expanding trade with the Roman world.

During Roman times, too, the first roads were built and the first market centres developed, the basic skeleton of the Suffolk we know today.

After the Romans left, international trade dwindled and industrial activity was mainly restricted to the village craftsman, but by the sixth century the Kingdom of East Anglia was developing and trade and industry with it. The Sutton Hoo treasures include evidence of imports from Scandinavia, the Rhincland and as far afield as the Mediterranean and this trade led to the development of Ipswich as a port. Recent finds confirm that Ipswich was a major centre of the Saxon pottery industry distributing its products throughout Britain.

The conversion of East Anglia to Christianity in the seventh century brought craftsmen and rare materials from the continent so that, by the Conquest, Suffolk was rich and prosperous, adding cloth and embroidery to its traditional exports.

During medieval times the economy continued to flourish. Increasing international trade led to the development of new ports at Dunwich, Beccles and Bungay. The flour milling, malting and brewing industries were developed to use locally grown cereals; tanning and glove-making to use local supplies of hides and skins; fishermen ventured out of the estuaries into the North Sea and even as far as Iceland; boats were being built at yards in Dunwich and Felixstowe, salt production and pottery continued to expand. This period also saw what might almost be called the foundation of our tourist industry, with the great pilgrimage sites in Bury St. Edmunds and Ipswich attracting large numbers of visitors.

We have seen that wool was being produced and marketed in Suffolk in Roman times but the woollen textile industry which derived from it deserves special mention as so many of our wonderful villages and market towns owed their prosperity to it.

Until the early Middle Ages spinning and weaving was essentially a cottage industry carried out throughout the land to meet local demand. The product was strong coarse cloth and the rich relied on imports for the finer qualities they wanted.

During the medieval period the production of high quality woollen broadcloth was developed and the swift-running, gravelly bottomed River Stour proved ideal for fulling mills. Increasing quantities of wool were imported from neighbouring counties to meet the growing demand.

To help the local industry to expand its range and output a heavy export duty was imposed on wool in 1347 and the immigration of craftsmen from the Low Countries, which had already started, was further encouraged.

Growing from the established centres along the Stour, South West Suffolk benefitted most from this policy – Sudbury, Lavenham, Long Melford, Hadleigh, Glemsford, Boxford, Nayland, Haverhill and Clare, among others, became cloth-making towns. Bury continued as a major market-place for buyers from London, with Ipswich as the main port for the export trade which extended to the Baltic, Russia, Spain, North Africa, France and Turkey as well as the Low Countries.

The broadcloth industry continued to flourish until the middle of the sixteenth century when lighter fabrics became more fashionable. The new 'bays & says' – fine serge type cloths – began to be manufactured and the Stour valley towns started to lose their trade.

So all good things come to an end. In 1700 an Act was passed to prohibit the import of printed cotton cloths from India in order to try and protect the home industry, but the growing importance of the modern mills in Yorkshire and Lancashire had disastrous results for the Suffolk weavers. There were more than 40,000 Suffolk people employed in the industry in the 1750's and the trade recession hit them hard. Much ingenuity was used to find work for them, some manufacturers turning more to hemp and flax, which had been grown locally since the Middle Ages, some to horsehair or coconut fibre, while the silk weavers of Spitalfields in London were encouraged to move to Sudbury, Haverhill and Glemsford where skilled workers were more readily available, more amenable and probably less well-paid than their traditional workforce. Another little known consequence of the decline of the cloth trade was the growth of straw-plaiting for hats. In 1851 there were some 2,000 women and girls working at home as straw-plaiters but this activity was shortlived and had died out by the 1890's.

So much for the cloth industry. Alongside it in the seventeenth and eighteenth centuries Suffolk farmers prospered too as more and more food was needed for the capital. Most clothiers had substantial farms and butter and cheese was exported to London from the medieval period until the eighteenth century at least. Defoe in his *Tour through the Whole Island of Great Britain* remarks that High Suffolk was 'famous for the best butter and perhaps the worst cheese in England'! It was to serve this thriving agricultural industry that the next wave of industrial development occurred.

The first iron foundry in the county was established in Ipswich by Robert Ransome in 1789 to make a new type of plough share he had invented. His company flourished as agricultural engineers of international repute producing the first lawn-mowers 150 years ago and Ransomes remain pre-eminent in this market today. Another branch of the business developed products for the railways and civil engineering, while at Leiston in 1849 Richard Garrett started the production of steam engines and boilers for agricultural use. It is a great joy to me that part of his factory – one of the first to use 'flow line' production methods – is being so well restored and is open to the public.

The abundance of grain had provided the raw materials for the flour miller and maltster for hundreds of years. The nineteenth century saw these processes develop to industrial scale. Nearly every town of any size would have had its mill, maltings and brewery, now larger units appeared and demand grew to outstrip the quantity of wheat and barley available. So the importation of cereals was necessary and Ipswich developed as a major destination for grain clippers from all over the world.

While grain products could be stored reasonably well from crop to crop, meat and fish needed to be processed in some way. Fish smoking and salting has been carried out near Lowestoft since early times and flourished until overtaken by the recent development of refrigeration and deep freeze techniques. Meat, too, was salted until these new processes led to the development of the large modern plants at Haverhill, Elmswell and Ipswich.

The growing sophistication of Suffolk's farmers led to another interesting development – the manufacture of artificial fertilisers using a phosphatic material, coprolite, the fossilised remains of prehistoric animal droppings, readily available in the Deben valley. Long after these supplies were exhausted the industry continued to flourish using imported raw materials. Another industrial 'first' for Suffolk was the factory opened in Lavenham in 1868 to process sugar beet; it was not very successful and the industry we know today has grown from the factory built in Ipswich in 1925.

Many of these more recent industrial ventures were given added impetus by the liberalisation of international trade in the early years of the last century – the growth of Lowestoft and Ipswich docks provided easy access for imported raw materials and the barge fleet working the East Coast provided cheap transport to the Port of London.

Alongside the industries which developed to use local agricultural products or supply farmers were a great variety of other ventures. Some, like the manufacture of gun-cotton at Stowmarket, no longer exist. Others have done well and are prosperous still – well-established printing companies moved out of London at the end of the last century because the militancy of the London unions was making their production uneconomic. Some chose Suffolk, Clays of Bungay, Clowes of Beccles and Cowells of Ipswich are respected throughout the world. One of the first ever plastics factories was established a hundred years ago for the manufacture of Xylonite at Brantham and is still a world leader. Tobacco was first processed in Ipswich nearly 200 years ago and cigars are still made there.

Why all this history? In the previous paragraphs I have endeavoured to show that there can hardly be a village in the county which has been unaffected by the growth of trade and industry. There remain many visible signs of our industrial past. Some – wind and tide mills, maltings, magnificent barns, old docks – we work hard to preserve. Others – obsolete power stations and gasholders, for example – we may not be so happy about. But we are lucky indeed that we do not have the legacy of slag heaps, derelict steel mills and vast factories suffered by those in the industrial Midlands and North.

There are other aspects of our medieval wealth of which we are justly proud – our legacy of noble and lovely churches, many fine houses, towns and villages with streets wide enough to accommodate markets, the fine parks in Ipswich were all made possible by the county's prosperity.

So where do we go from here? Developments during this century – and especially since the Second World War – point the way. As in the rest of Britain, we have seen the rise in importance of engineering and ship building followed by their relative decline; our grain based industries have been revolutionised by new technology so that while the county produces more flour, malt and animal feed than before they employ far fewer people, as does the printing industry; modern food processing has developed strongly. These trends seem likely to continue.

The 1939 war saw the revival of importance of the defence 'industry' due, as throughout early history, to our proximity to continental Europe – our air bases remain a major source of income and employment.

The county's ports are of the utmost importance to our economic future. We have seen that Ipswich and Lowestoft have been active since earliest times; the port of Felixstowe is a relative newcomer first becoming operational just over a hundred years ago. Recent years have seen dramatic development. Lowestoft, being Britain's most easterly port, is ideally suited for trade with Scandinavia, the Baltic and the Low Countries. Lowestoft benefited greatly from the development of the North Sea oil and gas industries, for which it has become a major service centre, helping to offset the effects of the recession in its famous fishing industry.

After World War II the far-sighed owners of Felixstowe port recognised its potential as a base for the new container trade – the necessary land was available near the port and could be developed more efficiently than in the old, congested, traditional docks elsewhere. Being privately owned it was outside the constraints of the dock labour legislation, but with a high degree of mechanisation only a relatively small labour force was required. Growth was rapid – in 1985 Felixstowe was the first port in the UK to handle more than half a million containers and the Trinity Terminal, opened in 1986 added 50% more capacity. It remains Britain's largest container handling port serving Europe, America, Africa, Australasia and the Middle and Far East. The 'million containers' milestone was passed in 1987 and the port is now embarking on yet another expansion programme.

Ipswich port, too, has taken full advantage of the new trading opportunities. By the outbreak of the Second World War it was handling a million tons of general cargo a year, by 1986 its trade had risen to four and a half million tons. New terminals have been developed on the West Bank of the Orwell and it is now the leading short-sea container port in the UK ranking fourth for worldwide container trade and handling a range of bulk cargoes as well.

These port developments have led to the growth of a wide range of ancilliary commercial and industrial businesses to service the ports themselves and the shipping and road transport companies that use them.

New sources of power have had a major impact. The discovery of North Sea oil and gas not only led to the growth of support services in the Waveney district but also to the demise of many small coal gas installations; the development of nuclear power has led to the construction of the first Sizewell station – now to be followed by Sizewell 'B', a big employer of construction workers for several years to come – and the closure of the coal-fired station at Ipswich.

Information technology is now of great importance to us.

The happy choice of Martlesham for the new site of British Telecom's Research Laboratories provides employment for hundreds of highly qualified scientists and technicians and gives Suffolk a world renowned centre of excellence of which we are justly proud. The use of these new technologies has enabled Ipswich to become established as a centre of national importance for the insurance industry providing employment just when it was needed for those displaced from the more traditional activities as they became less labour intensive.

Other 'high tec' industries have found ideal locations along the A45 corridor, especially at Bury St. Edmunds, and with smaller firms starting up in nearby villages. A less welcome factor is the growing concentration of the retail trade in Super-stores and Hypermarkets which is threatening the existence of the village shop.

The electrification of the main railway line to London and improvements to the trunk roads have made the county more accessible for commuters to the capital seeking cheaper housing. Easier communications attract small scale industry moving away from London to find cheaper factory sites and an adaptable labour force.

Though I believe the rate of change these developments have brought about may well slow down in the next few years as the 'South East Effect' spreads more widely throughout the country, I do not believe it will be reversed. The growing importance of continental markets will see to that.

What can we do to accommodate this growth of industrial activity without spoiling Suffolk as a fine place in which to live and work?

Clearly one of the most intrusive results of recent change has been the growth in heavy goods traffic on our roads. It is unfortunate that we missed the motorway building boom of the 1960s and 70s as motorways have proved more effective even than double carriageway trunk roads in keeping heavy lorries away from the town and village centres. It is probably now unlikely that the county will ever have any motorway mileage, so we should press for the continuing improvement of the primary road network and the construction of bypasses for towns and villages. As the rate of road improvement is largely controlled by central government a strong voice at Westminster is needed.

The population of the county – now in excess of 600,000 – is expected to grow to 650,000 before the end of the century; people are living longer and setting up house earlier. How can sufficient housing be provided?

These problems of traffic and population growth are tackled at several levels – the local councils of East Anglia, working together, take a view of the developments likely to take place in the region over the next twenty-five years, the County Council regularly reviews its strategic plan with which the district councils' local plans must comply. A very great deal of work is put into these plans by local government planning specialists and elected councillors alike. The procedure for introducing any significant changes or new plans allows plenty of time for consultation with interested bodies and the general public.

This planning procedure seems to me to be meticulously carried out considering the enormous problems the rapidly changing economy brings about. But there is, I believe, an inherent disadvantage in that the process is essentially 'top down' with parish councils being the last to be consulted.

In rural areas our parishes face a variety of problems. More cars mean less demand for bus and rail services while the more elderly still need public transport; houses occupied by week-enders rather than local families may result in fewer children needing places at the village school and less use being made of the village shop so both may be threatened with closure.

While parish councils do not have statutory powers in relation to planning decisions, I would like to see them playing a more positive role in the planning process and their views given more weight by the higher authorities.

I would like parish councils to initiate positive plans and not just react to the planning applications sent to them for comment. If our villages are to live they must be alive. They should again become centres of economic activity as they have been in the past. Fortunately the rapidly growing technologies of today make this possible without destroying those features of the countryside it is more desirable to preserve.

Parish councils know where 'infill' housing would be acceptable and may well feel that additional sites outside the historically defined village envelope could be developed. Their views should be actively sought and they should be encouraged to suggest sites for small businesses. Many people who live in the country – sometimes particularly those who have recently emigrated from towns – fear the development of industry. But if properly sited and appropriately selected the benefits should far outweigh the disadvantages – the new technologically based activities do not involve lorries thundering through the village street or the noise of heavy machinery disturbing the peace at all hours of the day and night. They may well prove less intrusive than modern farming! They will certainly bring more trade for the village shop and pub and provide additional employment opportunities close at hand for local people.

Tourism is another growth industry which can benefit our villages. On the estuaries and rivers the growth of yacht marinas and moorings provides new economic opportunity. Inland the interest in riding, walking and the countryside offers plenty of scope. Farmers are increasingly encouraged to diversify and villages can benefit from their development of holiday accommodation, nature trails, riding stables, and so on. I would like to see more of our villages – not just the well-known ones – actively promoting themselves as good places to visit.

Of course most of our economic activity is still located in the major towns and will remain so. There are still areas of derelict land near docks and railways which should be used for larger industrial operations in preference to green field sites. Our towns are not alone in suffering from traffic congestion and insufficient, or inconveniently sited car parks. Significant improvement takes many years to accomplish but should be given high priority. Difficult decisions have to be made – we should press hard to retain the finest of our urban buildings but accept that in adapting to change some of those less worthy should make way for new. If the centre of our towns is allowed to ossify more trade will move to sites near to the by-passes – encouraging even more urban sprawl – or move away from the county altogether.

My own company did not choose to join or contribute to any 'preservation' societies. We found them too negative in their approach – often ready to use their influence to prevent change, seldom prepared to offer constructive advice or to compromise. There are buildings in Ipswich today of no unique significance which have remained empty for years and will, I believe, eventually be demolished but the delay caused by this reactionary approach will have cost a great deal of money.

Other businessmen share my views and I think it is unfortunate that this antagonism has been allowed to develop. Trade and industry provides two thirds of the employment in the county, pays a quarter of the rates and together with agriculture provides all our wealth. Contrary to popular belief, the businessmen I know are as keen as anyone else to avoid 'spoiling' the surroundings in which we live as well as work. A more co-operative attitude on the part of the preservationists would surely benefit both parties.

The run-up to the twenty-first century will be greatly influenced by the unification of trade within the Common Market in 1992, which will increase the movement of goods among the member states. We have seen that Suffolk's ports are ideally situated to benefit and I expect their business to continue to increase, despite the construction of the Channel Tunnel.

The dramatic changes in information technology will make it even easier for firms to move out of overpriced locations in London and many will look to Suffolk as has happened in the past. Suffolk has many excellent 'high-tec' companies and research establishments now. I expect their numbers to increase providing higher-skilled grades of employment and better career prospects than previously available. Our schools and colleges are gearing-up to educate and train our young people for these new opportunities – I hope our youngsters will be encouraged to take advantage of them.

So, changes in Common Market policy and 'high-tech' developments, with the consequences of farm surpluses, the changing pattern of the retail trade and increasing leisure time will not pass Suffolk by. But, like equally dramatic changes in the past, they can be turned to our advantage. They should enable us to bring a new vitality to our villages and smaller towns; they will provide higher level employment opportunities for our young people as well as better services for the elderly.

If this is to be achieved without lasting damage to the fabric of the county we so much enjoy they must be integrated sympathetically.

I have made some suggestions as to how that this can be achieved. By a more positive involvement in planning by parish and town councils. By a positive involvement in county and district plans – at an early stage – by all interested representative bodies. By better co-operation between the amenity societies and the business community.

All change arouses fear. I have endeavoured to show that 'our' Suffolk is, in no small measure, a result of trading and industrial ventures of the past. I believe we should not fear the changes now upon us; but seize the new technologies as providing opportunity for improvements rather than presenting problems to be resisted at all costs.

My fear is not change, but apathy. Few structural changes are initiated by central government; most are planned, co-ordinated, encouraged or controlled by councils within the county itself. Yet seldom do more than 30% of the voters turn out at local government elections and only a much smaller proportion can name their representative on any of these local bodies.

With greater – and more positive – involvement in the planning processes we can go forward with confidence and my hope is that in fifty years time another writer will be able to say 'in the nineties our predecessors took full advantage of the new technology available to them while preserving the best of our historic legacy. We thank them for that.'

John Fitch was born at Mistley, Essex (but within sight of Suffolk where he has roots).

After reading History and Theology at Cambridge and training at Wells he was ordained (1947) and served for forty years in the pastoral/parish ministry in Suffolk, successively at Newmarket, Reydon, Brandon and Monks Eleigh. He was much involved in setting up the Suffolk Historic Churches Trust in 1974 and in its subsequent progress.

He was appointed an honorary Canon of St. Edmundsbury in 1975. He retired in 1987 and now lives at Great Yeldham close to the Suffolk border.

The Churches – and their Future

John Fitch

Every English county has churches of which it is, or ought to be, proud.

In today's secular world, an age of unparalleled intellectual, spiritual and moral confusion, they stand foursquare, mute witnesses to the unchanging glory of the God of Truth and Love – places where, however inadequately, his Word is proclaimed, his praises sung, and his Sacraments administered as of old. They illustrate, to those with eyes to see and knowledge to interpret, developing architectural styles, aesthetic tastes and liturgical fashions. And they mirror faithfully, because unselfconsciously, their locality's geology, building materials and techniques, its craftsmanship, industry and social structure, its history of prosperity or decline. For all these reasons, they are uniquely precious.

Whilst this is true of all counties, a handful, predominantly rural, are, by common consent, pre-eminent. Of these, Suffolk is not the least.

With almost exactly five hundred parish churches of medieval or earlier origin still remaining (out of 15,000 in England as as a whole), Suffolk shares with Norfolk the distinction of being the most heavily churched of all English counties.

A consequence of this density is that wherever in the county you may be, except perhaps in Breckland, you can never be more than two or three miles at most from an ancient church and rarely out of sight of one or more. Indeed it is said that from the roof of Wickham Market's octagonal tower (let alone the top of its spire!) with binoculars on a clear winter's day, fifty others can be seen.

These landmarks are a quintessential and ubiquitous feature of the quiet Suffolk landscape. Some, like Lavenham, Kersey and Stoke by Nayland, with their tall, heavily buttressed towers, command the undulating countryside for miles around. Others provide the focal point of the towns or villages they serve, whether crowning the village green like Long Melford, Cavendish and Monks Eleigh, or, like Clare, Hadleigh, Beccles, Mildenhall, or Sudbury's three handsome towers, serenely presiding over the bustle of a busy market town. Others again, shyly withdrawn, remote from village, hamlet, or even lane, often with only the manor house for neighbour (sometimes not even that), approached along a grassy path through a private park maybe, as at Sotterley, Euston, Ickworth or Little Glemham, or by a rough track across fields as at Badley, Carlton by Saxmundham, Chilton by Sudbury, Wangford near Brandon, Washbrook or Depden (tantalisingly observed from the A143 but unapproachable save roundabout on foot – and locked when you do get there!)

In a maritime county steeples serve as seamarks. As the endpapers of his valuable but long out of print *Suffolk Coast Garland* (London, Heath Cranton, 1928), Ernest R. Cooper reproduced engravings 'from the 1785 edition of the *English Pilot* of 1752, after Collins' *Coasting Pilot* of 1693'. They depict the Suffolk coast from various points offshore, sketching windmills, woods, lighthouses, beacons, hamlets, but, above all, church towers, with directions for navigation, e.g. 'Thus sheweth Loestoffe from the Red

Sand when the Church beareth North West' and (fascinating this, because Dunwich's last medieval church, All Saints, finally disappeared over the cliff in 1919) 'Thus sheweth Dunwich and Walderſwick when Dunwich Church bears NW two leags off. The shore ſide is white sandy cliff'.

To sail up the coast today from Felixstowe to Corton with only this old Pilot as guide would be exciting if hazardous. Some of the 1693/1785 seamarks have gone, but a noble succession of steeples would still be sighted – Orford, Aldeburgh, Walberswick, Southwold, Covehithe, (possibly) Benacre, Kessingland, Pakefield (now within yards of the cliff top), Lowestoft (St. Margaret), and finally Corton, with the dramatic silhouette of its ruined nave.

And if, further, on a favourable tide, you felt disposed to sail in turn up the estuaries of the Stour, Orwell, Deben, Alde and Blyth, you would be rewarded with some of Suffolk's most enchanting prospects – Erwarton Church surveying the lower reaches of the Stour, Ramsholt the Deben, Iken on its promontory up the Alde and, most splendid of all, Blythburgh riding majestically at anchor overlooking the Blyth valley, the battlefield of Bulcamp where in 654 the East Anglian king Anna was slain, his remains allegedly brought to be buried where the church now stands. Finally, having sailed up the Orwell to the Port of Ipswich, you would glimpse that impressive string of grimy black beauties, the flint dockside churches of St. Clement, St. Mary Quay and St. Peter, all now sadly redundant, overshadowed and all but hidden by gaunt waterside warehouses and offices and throttled by traffic, but still bravely witnessing to Ipswich's medieval prosperity, lately renewed.

We could go on indefinitely, so integral to the Suffolk scene are its churches. How unimaginably bald it would be without them.

Those earlier churches, especially, which have retained, unspoilt, their characteristic texture, of rubble, knapped flint, dressed stone, brick, plaster, timber, pantiles, thatch, of local crag or septaria, reflecting vernacular building materials and methods available hereabouts in medieval times, speak to us endearingly and eloquently, with a strong Suffolk accent. A prime example of texture, from so many, is Ixworth Thorpe. Others are Great Livermere, Hoo, Cretingham, Wantisden, Barsham, Shelley, Withersdale, Little Wenham, Thornham Parva, Fritton – all miraculously unspoilt and unsophisticated.

Fourteen years ago, when launching the Suffolk Historic Churches Trust (SHCT) with a memorable lecture in the Theatre Royal, Bury St. Edmunds, the late Kenneth (Lord) Clark, leading art historian of his day, told us that it was Suffolk churches visited on schoolboy cycle rides from his father's home at Sudbourne which first aroused his interest in Gothic architecture. Referring, by way of examples, to Woodbridge and Framlingham, with their grand flint flushwork towers, and to Ufford's prodigious font cover, he went on to make a bold claim.

'Suffolk churches,' he said, 'are (with the possible exception of the Wash churches) the most beautiful in England.'

In saying this, Lord Clark was not abusing his enormous authority to gratify us with a vague generalisation about Suffolk churches in their entirety! Rather, he was referring specifically to the churches of our Golden Age, the century and a half beginning about 1370 and concluding with the Reformation. Thanks largely to the boom in the broadcloth trade in South and West Suffolk and that in the herring industry on the coast, but also in part to the munificence of noble, and humbler, benefactors (Wingfields, de la Poles, Howards, Drurys, Felbriggs, Bardolphs, Cloptons, Martyns, Springs and de Veres among them), this was the period which saw the rebuilding, enlargement and refurnishing on a magnificent scale of so many of our parish churches in that Perpendicular style which represents the peculiarly English contribution to the sum total of European architecture.

It is scarcely possible to exaggerate and totally impossible in the space at our disposal to do more than hint at the richness of this marvellous achievement, even diminished as it is by the iconoclastic destruction of most of the medieval glass.

Suffolk Perpendicular was the culmination of long centuries of almost uninterrupted church building, adaptation, enlargement and re-building, beginning with the first preaching of the Gospel here by Felix from Burgundy and Fursey from Ireland back in the seventh century and the conversion and consolidation that ensued.

Despite the significant fact, firmly established by Norman Scarfe, that some 417 of our 500 surviving medieval churches are recorded in Domesday Book as already existing in 1086 – more than in any other county and averaging, he says, one church to every 150 of the then population – relatively little pre-Conquest church building has survived in Suffolk. The main examples are the lower stage of Debenham's massive square tower, exhibiting characteristic long and short masonry in the quoins, and an uncertain number of our forty or so round towers – certainly Holy Trinity, Bungay, and Little Bradley, and perhaps also Herringfleet, Hengrave and Wissett. Round towers are notoriously hard to date with precision.

The majority of the Domesday churches have been rebuilt, many of them time and time again, but 200 or so still retain identifiable Norman features, chiefly doorways, ranging from rustic simplicity (Ubbeston, Milden) to great sophistication (Westhall, Wissington, Wissett, Great Bricett), some with carved tympana like the tree of life(?) at

Wordwell. Notable Norman fonts survive at Wantisden, Preston and St. Peter's Ipswich.

For three outstanding examples illustrating gradual development from the twelfth to the fifteenth centuries, go to Westhall, Polstead and Lakenheath, prepared to spend plenty of time at each, with help from Cautley, Pevsner or Scarfe (or at Lakenheath from the late John Munday's excellent and scholarly guide), unravelling their complex history.

With the thirteenth century came the revolutionary discovery of the pointed arch, at once outmoding Norman and signalling the arrival of Early English Gothic, seen at its most typical in the vaulted North chapel of Mildenhall and the triple lancets of Rumburgh tower.

With accelerating architectural daring and the elaboration of new stained glass techniques combining to create a demand for ever larger and more elaborate windows, the austere elegance of Early English had by degrees given way by the beginning of the fourteenth century to the style aptly called Decorated or Geometrical, most obviously exemplified in elaborate reticulated or curvilinear window tracery. It is delightfully seen in a variety of forms at Icklingham All Saints, Cotton, Redgrave, Burstall, Gazeley and Westhorpe and, notably, in the chancels of Mildenhall and Dennington, and the nave and aisles of Orford. Cotton is perhaps our best complete 'Dec.' church but a 'Perp.' double hammerbeam roof and clerestory were added a century later, causing one arcade to list alarmingly to starboard.

And so we return in the later fourteenth century, following the Black Death, to Perpendicular, the crown of the Gothic achievement, Suffolk's Golden Age. Essentially rectangular it is, perpendicular *and* horizontal, giving us the L-shaped South elevations seen, typically, at Blythburgh, Southwold, Denston, Lowestoft, Woodbridge, Wingfield,

Stowlangtoft, Long Melford and Lavenham. Most of these were built continuously, all of a piece – Lavenham, the most notable exception, being sumptuous 'Perp.' wrapped, including its grand North and South chantry chapels, round an earlier 'Dec.' chancel. In most, too, with Lavenham again the exception, there is no structural separation between nave and chancel (partitioned though they were internally by a rood screen). In these, a clerestory runs the entire length West to East, giving maximum light to the roof.

And what roofs! They are one of Suffolk's greatest glories. It is acknowledged by the best authorities, Francis Bond, Cautley, Pevsner, Clark, that in this field our county stands supreme, unchallenged in England, even in Europe. Marvellous diversity (single and double hammer beams, arch-braced tie beams, in every kind of ingenious combination), sheer technical brilliance and rich carved (and formerly painted) decoration on hammer beams, cornices, wall plates, spandrils, corbels and bosses, are all to be found in 'Perp.' naves, aisles and chancels. Spectacular examples are Mildenhall (Kenneth Clark's 'cockpit of angels'), Lakenheath, St. Mary's, Bury St. Edmunds, St. Margaret's, Ipswich, Framlingham, Blythburgh, Walsham le Willows, Southwold, Denston, Grundisburgh, Earl Stonham, Woolpit, Worlingworth, and Long Melford Lady Chapel, while for sheer daring, Needham Market is in a class by itself.

'Perp.' churches abound, too, in wonderful woodwork not only in roofs but in screens, benches, stalls with misericords, pulpits, font covers and doors.

Externally, besides a profusion of noble towers, porches and clerestories, what is most distinctive in our fifteenth century churches is the wondrous display so many of them afford of the peculiarly East Anglian art of flint flushwork, an intricate black and white mosaic of dressed stone and knapped flint, of spellbinding virtuosity in such examples as Gipping, Southwold, Lavenham, Kersey, Long Melford and, very notably, Eye and Laxfield towers.

Space does not permit more than a glance at post-Reformation churches, of which, because the Middle Ages had served us so well, we have so few – but Euston, an elegant Wren-like rebuilding of 1676 on the medieval plan and foundations, and the delightfully intact 1745 classical chancel at Shotley, deserve special mention. Pride of place in this period, however, should go to Dissenting chapels, of which Suffolk boasts three outstanding early examples, mid seventeenth century rustic Walpole, looking outside like a cottage, and the highly sophisticated Unitarian meeting houses at Friars Street, Ipswich (1700) and Churchgate Street, Bury (1711), all three miraculously preserved inside and out. Also, Bury Roman Catholics have a handsome neo-Classical church of 1837, St. Edmund's, Westgate Street, complete with box pews. This now incorporates its tiny, charming predecessor, the Blessed Sacrament Chapel of 1762, itself perhaps the earliest surviving RC place of worship to be licensed in this county in post-penal times (under the Act of 1791).

As Suffolk had been fortunate in the coincidence of its fifteenth century prosperity with the Perpendicular achievement, it was hardly less so that, in the nineteenth century, when it had become an agricultural backwater, a fortunate combination of tenacious, old fashioned conservatism with apathy, neglect or sheer poverty of local resources spared so many of our churches from the ruthless though well meaning 'restoration' then so fashionable, to delight a later generation more appreciative of their unspoilt atmospheric quality, so redolent of classical, pre-Tractarian, Prayer Book churchmanship. Examples abound – Cretingham, Badley, Shelland, Withersdale, Gipping, Dennington in East Suffolk, and in West,

Denston, Barnardiston, Cowlinge, Kedington and Brent Eleigh.

To take a positive view of the nineteenth century more in keeping with the current appreciation of Victoriana, for an instructive example of what drastic 'restoration' in 1863, amounting practically to rebuilding, could do to a medieval church, go to Brome, near Eye. There is no lack of others.

The last hundred years have not seen the erection of many first rate churches in Suffolk. The best are suburban – in Ipswich, monumental red brick St. Bartholomew's (High Church) and St. John's (Low Church), both of the 1890's, with perhaps Munro Cautley's St. Augustine's (1927) and All Hallows (1938), and at Felixstowe the (unfinished) neo-Perp. concrete St. Andrew's built to celebrate Parliament's rejection of the 1928 Prayer Book. New churches apart, Stephen Dykes Bower's triumphalist, ultra-conservative extension of St. Edmundsbury Cathedral, still incomplete, is unquestionably this century's finest church building achievement in Suffolk.

The twentieth century has in fact been much more concerned with the task of preserving old churches than with building new ones.

The Suffolk Historic Churches Trust

It was in the immediate post-war years, with a huge backlog of church repairs interrupted by hostilities, that we began to become aware of the size and urgency of this task. Nationwide, the establishment in 1952 of the Historic Churches Preservation Trust (HCPT) helped to focus public attention and to raise and distribute money to assist and encourage hard-pressed parishes. Even so, Suffolk lagged behind and two more decades were to pass before we were able to set up our own county Trust. And it was not until 1977 that long awaited and desperately needed State aid for historic churches first became available.

In the meantime, mounting inflation brought escalating labour costs, doubly discouraging for a Church faced with domestic problems enough of its own, dwindling congregations and limited resources of money and manpower. The need for massive repair programmes in so many parishes was brought home to hard-pressed clergy, churchwardens and PCCs (which continued in law, as they still do, to bear the prime responsibility for the maintenance, repair and insurance of their church fabrics) by the implementation of the Inspection of Churches Measure, 1955, under which every parish church must be inspected by a competent diocesan architect every five years. The resulting Quinquennial Survey Reports, though not always uniform in their criteria, built up an invaluable picture of the scale and cost of work needed to put Suffolk's churches into sound repair. In these years before the advent of SHCT and State aid, it is truly remarkable how much was achieved by the heroic efforts of 'the few', often in tiny rural parishes with vast churches, to finance and carry out the necessary work. But these were a minority and in too many parishes little or nothing was done and things went from bad to worse. The situation was exacerbated by the continuing depopulation of rural areas, the grouping of more and more parishes together, and the disappearance of so many of the old squires alive to their financial responsibilities for 'their' churches.

It was in these circumstances, with a sharpening public awareness of the gravity of these problems and the shadow of redundancy or ruin hanging over so many (often distinguished) churches that a massive piece of church legislation, the Pastoral Measure, was eventually enacted in 1968, setting up the complex structures and procedures which have since governed all such questions.

It would be unnecessarily tedious to attempt to describe them here in detail. Suffice it to say that when, in Suffolk, on the initiative of a PCC finding or believing itself unable any longer to maintain its church, a declaration of redundancy is approved by the Bishop on the advice of the Diocesan Pastoral Committee, the matter goes to the Church Commissioners, who consult their Redundant Churches Advisory Board as to the quality of the church concerned, whether or not it is judged worthy to be vested in the Redundant Churches Fund. Failing that, in a three-year waiting period, a suitable alternative use has to be sought for it, with a view to a sale. Failing any such use, in the very last resort, it must be demolished and the site sold, part of the proceeds going to the Redundant Churches Fund. This ultimate solution has so far only befallen two Suffolk churches, both in Lowestoft; St. John's and St. Peter's, both 19th century buildings of little merit.

In the twenty years since the Pastoral Measure became law, 40 Suffolk churches, 34 of them of actual parish church status, have been declared redundant. Of these, three are at the time of writing (April 1988) awaiting a final decision as to their fate.

Of the remaining 37, fourteen are vested in the Redundant Churches Fund (Akenham, Badley, Bungay St. Mary, Chilton, Claydon, Ellough, Icklingham All Saints, Ipswich St. Mary Quay, Little Wenham, Rickinghall Superior, Sapiston, South Elmham All Saints, Sudbury St. Peter, and Wordwell), together with one ruin (Stanton St. John) and two towers (Covehithe and Newton, with other parts of both churches, the rest being retained in use for worship in both cases) and five in the similar Ipswich Historic Churches Trust (St. Clement's, St. Lawrence's, St. Nicholas', St. Peter's and St. Stephen's).

The preservation for posterity of these nineteen medieval churches, in good repair and with reasonable public access, is thus assured and they may be, and most of them are, in occasional use for acts of worship, concerts and exhibitions, particularly where, as at St. Peter's, Sudbury, there is strong local interest and support. The RCF, funded jointly by Church and State, is a wholly admirable body, with an excellent record and a sound philosophy of economical repair and maintenance.

Of the remaining eighteen so far declared redundant, most have been, or are being, sold: six (Braiseworth, Debach, Mickfield, Rishangles, Shipmeadow and Ubbeston) for conversion into houses; two, Benacre and Ickworth, to Sir John Gooch, Bart., and the Marquess of Bristol, respectively, for private maintenance as monuments or domestic chapels, and the rest for various other similar purposes. Alternative uses are hard to find and seldom wholly satisfactory.

This melancholy stream of redundant churches would undoubtedly have become a flood had it not been for two events in the 1970's, which together gave new heart to many hard-pressed parishes and chapel trustees, enabling them to 'hold the line'.

The first was the establishment in 1974 of the Suffolk Historic Churches Trust. With the Duke of Grafton as Chairman and a strong, representative and active body of Trustees, it rapidly became a force to be reckoned with, attracting enthusiastic and generous support, not only from private individuals but in annual grants from the County and District Councils, which have proved invaluable. These, with a series of imaginative fund raising events, culminating in six spectacularly successful sponsored bicycle rides, (in which our Trust pioneered the way for other counties to follow), have enabled it to give grants and encouragement totalling to date (April 1988) no less than £730,000 to 395 churches and chapels. In many cases, where churches have phased their repairs, we have given a whole succession of grants and, in gratitude, many PCCs have become corporate members of the Trust.

From the outset, besides raising and distributing funds and giving encouragement and, where needed, advice, the Trust has set out to foster interest, knowledge and enthusiasm for the cause of Suffolk historic churches and chapels. This it has done, and is doing, by a series of publications, exhibitions and study days as well as by lectures at its well attended AGMs.

The second event of the 1970s was, of course, the beginning of State Aid for historic churches and chapels in 1977. Suffolk was among the first counties to take full advantage of it. In the ten years to April, 1988, Suffolk churches and chapels had received altogether an astonishing total of £4,507,139 in taxpayers' money towards the cost of essential fabric repairs.

State aid, now channelled through the Historic Buildings and Monuments Commission (English Heritage), is not of course (and quite rightly) granted unconditionally and must be matched, in whatever proportion, by the recipients' own efforts. The average percentage at the time of writing is 40% but occasional grants have been made in very exceptional circumstances (i.e. where the church's importance is great and local resources meagre) up to 80% or even higher.

Here is one example, admittedly altogether exceptional, of the combined effect of the SHCT and of State aid on one tiny Suffolk parish. Denston in SW Suffolk has a total present adult population of 82 and shares its Rector with larger, neighbouring parishes. Ten years ago, its marvellous fifteenth century church was in a state of extreme dilapidation such as can now scarcely be imagined. Redundant?

No. Under very strong and persistent pressure, and encouragement, from the Trust, and with the support of the Diocese, a Restoration Appeal was launched in 1981, with strong local support, and repairs begun. They went steadily ahead, in phases. By February, 1988, with the work all but complete, Denston's Hon. Treasurer was able to report that, in the seven years since the appeal began, the parish *itself*, by direct giving and a series of special events, had raised no less than £37,849; grants (other than State aid) received included £9,500 from HCPT, £14,100 from SHCT; £2,500 from the Diocese; and from other outside sources nearly £20,000; while State aid over the seven years had totalled the astounding figure of £232,225. At an overall cost exceeding £300,000, Denston Church is now in excellent repair and all bills paid – a stupendous achievement by any standard.

Denston is obviously exceptional in *every* way but it does illustrate how the Trust and State aid between them have brought new hope to all who value our historic churches.

The Future

It is not easy to generalise truthfully and with confidence about our own times, even in this restricted field. Besides the two sources of encouragement just referred to, others are not lacking.

Suffolk has many 'live' parishes with expanding congregations, especially perhaps in suburbs. In recent years, two medieval churches, Kesgrave and Rushmere St. Andrew have had to be enlarged, a number of others (e.g. Westerfield, Barham and Reydon) to build annexes. Many parishes have undertaken major re-ordering schemes to adapt their churches to changing liturgical and social needs. (This, itself a healthy sign of life, needs, in an ancient church, to be tackled with extreme caution and sensitivity, as has been done so successfully at Chattisham and Ixworth – otherwise a beautiful and historic interior can be irretrievably wrecked and its atmosphere lost). Also, lay and part-time, locally ordained and non-stipendiary ministry is being developed, easing the burden of full-time clergy in multiple benefices. And ecumenical goodwill is resulting in more churches being shared.

Finally, on the credit side, is the immense amount of public interest in and concern for old churches and their history, much of it seemingly deriving from a kind of Betjemanesque nostalgia, and manifesting itself in a flood of relevant literature, such as the innumerable excellent guide books produced by Roy Tricker, the David Bellamy of Suffolk churches. (Would that every casual 'church crawler' put a realistic thank offering in the fabric fund box. Many do.)

On the debit side are an uncertain and varying number of (mostly) very small rural parishes with tiny, dwindling, elderly congregations and meagre resources, struggling desperately to meet insistent and ever increasing demands upon them, however justified, from the Diocese, to say nothing of the requirements of the latest Architect's Quinquennial. All this is compounded by problems of sacriligious vandalism and theft. Thus, often on police advice, many churches are kept locked day and night – surely a retrograde step. Locking churches in daytime is defeatist and rarely justifiable. Increased vigilance is the answer. And some risks must be taken.

Is it surprising that in these circumstances, *despite* SHCT and HCPT encouragement and State aid (sometimes refused), opting for redundancy often seems the only solution?

Sometimes a public parish meeting before the final PCC decision can arouse local support, tip the balance, and win the day. It is always worth a try. But, even so, the trickle of redundancies seems likely, alas, to continue.

So what of the long-term future?

A valid point, strongly urged in the report of a recent working party on Tourism and Churches, is that whereas in pre-Reformation times churches were in daily use, not only for worship but for every kind of communal activity, secular or sacred, so it ought to be again now. Instead of being open only for one hour a week on Sundays, they should, where feasible, be much more widely used by the whole community – as well as accessible and welcoming to tourists.

In recent years, many churches *have* in fact been much more widely used than ever before, at least since the Middle Ages – for concerts, recitals, flower festivals, exhibitions, drama, lectures and harvest suppers even. This is all to the good. No-one wants them to become mere museums. BUT . . .

We must get our priorities right. A parson, himself a woefully inadequate but convinced Christian believer, may be forgiven for a gentle reminder that, in the last analysis, churches are functional buildings, designed and consecrated to the glory of the living God of all life, as places where his people, the *living* Church, assembles for worship, prayer and thanksgiving, the sacraments and the 'rites of passage' – christenings, weddings, funerals. That must never be lost sight of. It is the key to the future.

In Soviet Russia and Communist China, where for so long churches were closed or turned over to *purely* secular uses or as museums, people are flocking back to worship God in them, rediscovering there a faith which makes sense of all life and experience.

In Suffolk, may there soon likewise arise, in a re-united Church, a new generation of Felixes, Furseys and Botolphs to proclaim afresh a basic, simplified, relevant, coherent Gospel. And may Suffolk's marvellous churches, old and new, regain their central place in the lives and affections of its people.

An index of Suffolk churches appears on pp 6–7.

Paul Jennings was born in Leamington, grew up in the family home town of Coventry where he went to King Henry VIII School, moving to Douai School at 15. Worked at GEC testing Post Office equipment for 'decibel gain' although didn't at first know what a decibel was. The jobs column had demanded a Higher Certificate, his was in Latin and Greek. All his companions had Physics. An oversight, so they moved him to publicity. Called up before the war he eventually became a Lieutenant in the Royal Signals. In India, if that counts.

After the war he wrote film strips for the Central Office of Information about British carpets, British dentists, British everything. After a brief spell in advertising he became the Observer's first and last humour (i.e. not satire) columnist with *Oddly Enough* from 1949 to 1966. This was decanted into 14 Oddly *books*, to which are added a novel *And Now For Something Exactly The Same*, three children's books, two documentaries (*The Living Village* and *Companion to Britain*); edited *The English Difference* and *The Book of Nonsense*. Much BBC work, was a founder member of *Face the Music* panel. Sings in the London Philharmonic Choir, now lives in Orford after 28 years in East Bergholt.

Plato's Suffolk

Paul Jennings

I went down yesterday to the harbour of Felixtoft, where our river Storblythen runs into the sea, for the festival of the goddess Anglia Kallista, to make our annual offering to thank her for the gifts of order and beauty which she bestows on us. As we were returning along the road – that is Polemarchus of East Bergholt, Nicias of Bury and his son Nicephoros, Cleitophon of Little Cornard and Euthydemus the Ipswichian together with Glaucon of Halesworth – we were hailed by Adeimantus, who had walked some way towards us. We had all been invited to dine with him, and afterwards watch the fireworks on this festival night.

We were surprised to see Thrasymachus of Bildeston with him. 'Why, Thrasymachus,' said Nicias, 'what a surprise! Did you not say, when we met in the jostling crowd at Felixtoft, that the continuance of the festival no longer gave you any pleasure, since the presence at it of so many visitors in their cars had made it quite different from the purely local gathering of farmers and fishermen, the traditional inhabitants of our region, which it was when we were young men?'

'That is true,' replied Thrasymachus. 'Nor do I think our

friend Adeimantus will be able to offer us as inspiring a view of the fireworks as would have been possible from the very same hilltop, on which his ancestral home stands, a mere fifty years ago, when they would have been seen against the perfect background of a dark, velvety, silent night (since, as you know, the festival of the goddess is always held on the day before the new moon). They would not, as now, be rivalled by the brilliant lights necessitated by continuous industrial activity. Indeed, not only Felixtoft but all our towns – many, indeed, of our larger villages – now project upon the night sky an unnatural orange glow which serves as a constant reminder that there is no longer a distinction between the country and the town.'

'It was I who persuaded Thrasymachus to join our gathering,' said Adeimantus. 'As we all saw, our friend Socrates was a participant in the celebration of the goddess, and when he saw gathered in one place persons from so many parts of our beloved Suffolk, and indeed beyond it, he yielded to my entreaty that he should join us at dinner, where we might agree on what new things should be admitted and what old things abandoned. For I am sure,' he added with a sly nod at Thrasymachus, 'that not all would be agreed that the answer in both cases should be "none at all", as our friend Thrasymachus would seem to believe.'

'That is certainly true,' said Thrasymachus.

'I came to meet you on the road,' said Adeimantus, 'thinking that Socrates would already be with you, and I should esteem it an honour to escort so famous a philosopher the last few steps to my house. But I perceive he is not.'

Just then the servant of Agathon came running up and told us that his master, finding himself next to Socrates, had waxed so eloquent over his joy at the award of Best Kept Village to the place where he lived and served on the parish council that Socrates had agreed to visit it, coming to our dinner by a roundabout route; he asked forgiveness of Adeimantus for the lateness of his arrival which this would cause and begged him not to delay but to start without him.

'That is just what I should expect of Agathon,' said Thrasymachus. 'He is a newcomer to Suffolk, and has been here only seventeen years. The house in which he lives was quite new when he came. Now his one desire is to prevent any more being built, and to ensure that no further changes are made.'

'But tell me, Thrasymachus, is it not true that you yourself do not wish any changes made?' We turned in surprise, to see Socrates and Agathon, who had joined our group unnoticed during this speech of Thrasymachus.

'It did not take us long,' said Socrates with a smile. 'It was clear to me, even without getting out of Agathon's car, that no village could be better kept than his.'

'Welcome, Socrates,' said Adeimantus. 'Now that you have joined us and heard what Thrasymachus has to say, should I not ask him in what way Agathon's desire for his village to remain unchanged is in some way inferior to his own exactly similar desire for his own village?'

At this Thrasymachus looked angry and said 'Two reasons occur to me immediately, and doubtless I could think of many more. In the first place I was born in the house in my village where my father was born and his father before him, in the days when it was still a farm, albeit in a village, not a moated farm standing remotely in the gently undulating fields which are a unique feature of our beloved landscape. In the second place, his conception of neatness is a suburban one which would have seemed absurd in my village when I was a child there, when the footpaths were separated from the roads by wandering grass, not by suburban kerbs; when houses in the true Suffolk pink, made from limewash and Venetian red and aged by many rains and suns, had not been bedizened in coats of Snowcem;

when all the people in the village were known to each other, and it was a place lived and worked in, and therefore had a living and unconsidered untidiness, instead of the deplorable neatness which is nowadays rewarded by the erection of a village sign of equally deplorable quaintness.'

'For my part,' said Nicias, 'it seems to me the question is not whether one man's love for Suffolk is superior or inferior, or indeed whether it is possible to measure such things, but rather what kind of Suffolk should be preserved for future men to love, in whatever way.'

'That is certainly what we must decide in order to live properly together,' said Socrates, 'but I see the wife of our host Adeimantus beckoning to us from her threshold, lest we delay further here and the meats be spoiled. Let us continue our discussion after doing justice to them.'

It was indeed an excellent repast. There remained plenty of good Bruisyard, Kelsale, Finn Valley and other Suffolk wines, and when Adeimantus had told his cup-bearer to see that ours were replenished, Socrates began: 'Would you have us believe, then, that he loves Suffolk best who loves it as it was when you were a child, Thrasymachus?'

'That is so, Socrates.'

'But if I understood you rightly, this Suffolk has already to some extent disappeared.'

'It certainly has, Socrates.'

'But can a man love something which does not exist?'

'You think to have trapped me nicely, Socrates. But suppose I say that I love the old parts of Suffolk and detest the new.'

'Do you include, among the new, the new *people*, Thrasymachus?'

'No. I was but jesting when I spoke so to Agathon before our dinner. He is my friend. Do we not play golf together at Aldeburgh?'

'Is it the case, then, that if a tyrant were to seize power in our country and decree that five hundred houses should be built on Aldeburgh golf course, you and he would make common cause against this?'

'Certainly, Socrates. And not only if it were the golf course. Five hundred new houses *anywhere* in Suffolk, huddled together too close, with gardens of inconvenient and unnatural shapes, often like slices of pie when the knife has slipped, would be totally out of keeping with the character of our beloved county. Indeed, you may see an extreme example of this at Haverhill.'

'You would agree, then, that there is a quality unique to Suffolk which is due in very large measure to the long pastoral centuries, gradually evolving, in contrast to the bewildering and sudden changes of our own day? Would it not then be necessary to have a class of persons admitted by all to be qualified to ordain how much, and no further, the demands of our modern age should be met?'

'That is certainly so, Socrates. And it follows from what I said previously that this class of persons, the Planners, should be quite innocent of the remotest connection with the building industry?'

'That seems to me one thing on which we are agreed,' said Socrates. 'Tell me, Polemarchus,' (for he had observed that Polemarchus of East Bergholt was becoming increasingly agitated and could scarcely refrain from interrupting), 'would you agree that while there are a finite number of features that could be described as "old" in Suffolk, but an infinite number of "new" possibilities, and since men as diverse in origin as Thrasymachus and Agathon are united in wanting to preserve the old, in whatever manner they conceive it, the Planners should have the power to decree the level below which the "old" features should not be reduced; for once an "old" feature has disappeared it has gone for ever?'

'That may be so, Socrates,' said Polemarchus, 'but permit me, Socrates, to attempt to turn the tables by questioning *you*. Is it not true that the population of Suffolk in 1901 was 384,291, in 1981 578,000, in 1986 610,000, and that the rate of increase, some 6,000 a year, is itself increasing?'

'I have no doubt that your figures are correct, Polemarchus,' said Socrates with a smile.

'I myself moved to Suffolk from the capital of our country, where I still work every day,' said Polemarchus. 'I moved soon after the major part of the A12 became dual-carriageway and used to drive up every day, although since the electrical trains have greatly reduced the time taken from Manningtree (if not, alas, the price of the tickets) I now go by train. I am therefore myself one of the newcomers. Would Thrasymachus have me return to the metropolis? At least neither he nor anyone else could reproach me for spoiling the appearance of the village by building a new house, as he did Agathon. For what brought me there in the first place was the chance to buy one at least four hundred years old.'

'I can quote figures from 1901 as well as Polemarchus,' said Thrasymachus. 'Then there were nearly a million and a half agricultural employees in our entire country, now there are barely 140,000. The influx here of new persons must therefore be entirely composed of those who wish merely to enjoy the Suffolk landscape which past agricultural generations have made without themselves being economically involved in it.'

At this Cleitophon, who had hitherto remained silent, said quietly 'Like all here present, I greatly desire a situation, arrived at logically and without advantage to any particular party, in which all were agreed as to what old things should be preserved in Suffolk, and what new ones prevented; and what encouraged. But I would make two observations – firstly, that chance or luck or "the way things are" is bound to enter into our deliberations; and secondly, that the farmers whom Thrasymachus would seem to regard as the custodians and only rightful inhabitants of Suffolk have themselves changed the landscape considerably from the one which, if I do not mistake them, such welcome neighbours as Polemarchus and Agathon regard as ideal. For from my house on a ridge I can see, to one side, the edge of a new, highly technical industrial complex no doubt giving employment to many persons, and on the other a landscape where hedges have disappeared, crops are gathered from huge fields by huge machines, and the sound of bird-song is rarely unaccompanied by the sound of a tractor, a chainsaw, or some other machine. Harvest stooks have been replaced by huge toilet-rolls of straw, old barns by new silo towers. Yet it remains a *beautiful* landscape, with enough of the past about it to make me appreciate it and wish to preserve it. I was, as it happens, born in Suffolk, although I am by trade a hand weaver who sells bright rugs to Sweden, Rumania and America.'

There was a general murmur of approval at this speech of Cleitophon's, but now Euthydemus the Ipswichian spoke, somewhat angrily. 'I should like to return to the claim made by Polemarchus that he may claim a kind of artistic virtue merely by buying an old house. Is he then saying that no artistic or educated person would wish to live in a new house? Is he aware that hopeless nostalgia for a rustic past, which goes with a pseudo-aristocratic contempt not merely for "trade" but for science itself, is the basic cause of our country's decline relative to such unlikely rivals as Japan?'

'We should remember, Euthydemus,' said Socrates, 'that Japan is, more like us than, let us say, America, a country which also has many ancient yet still cherished traditions. Would you then say, that in order to compete or indeed survive, we must abandon our love of a rustic past?'

'Certainly we must, Socrates,' replied Euthydemus. 'It is not relevant to our discussion whether or not I was born in

Suffolk. It must suffice to say that I live in Ipswich because I like the life of a town, especially if like Ipswich it possesses a theatre (where the performances may often give more pleasure than those to be seen at the much-vaunted National Theatre given by its dramatic civil servants) and a renovated concert hall; for towns also are a vital part of Suffolk –'

Here Euthydemus was interrupted by Thrasymachus, who said 'Ipswich isn't what it was in Defoe's time, when he said it was airy, clean and well-governed. Now it is merely a playground for developers like the rest of Suffolk. If you want a less spoiled Suffolk town, Bungay, Eye, Beccles, Southwold, Framlingham –' but here he was silenced by looks from the company, and Euthydemus continued:

'It seems to me – and I beg you all to believe that I do not wish to boast in this matter although my words may make it appear so – that it is possible for me, surrounded by so many self-confessed lovers of the past, to speak for a class of people without whom our entire country would be worrying not about such minor issues as the preservation of the old but about how to get enough to eat. It has long been known that persons such as Thrasymachus, indeed all of us, could not live as we do without possessing motor cars, although none of us apparently would care to live in a town where they are manufactured. But now it goes further. My firm, in the hi-tech electronic field, is concerned with matters of the next century. I moved it here because this is where we look to Europe. Why should we return from work in the future to homes built three centuries in the past? Are we to ask our architects to build old houses for us, if such a thing were possible?'

'You are right, Euthydemus,' said Socrates, 'to remind us that we cannot consider the problem of the future identity of Suffolk, let alone its continuity with its unique past, in isolation from the rest of our country (for did not our

Anglia give its name to all of it up to its boundaries with Scotland and Wales?). Modern mobility has meant that almost anyone can live almost anywhere. But I would ask you –'

Here Thrasymachus interrupted Socrates. 'We need look no further than Sizewell to see that our local interests do not concern the metropolis, where I do not doubt that no one knows or cares that as a result of it, and also because of extra staff needed to deal with planning applications not necessarily connected with it (though some are) increasing by 15% each year, the rates of the district in which it is situated have risen 42.3% in one year. I apologise for interrupting you, Socrates, but I feel that all should know these facts.'

'You are certainly right, Thrasymachus,' said Socrates. 'I was about to ask Euthydemus, knowing how hard and intensely he works, how he achieves the relaxation now known to be absolutely necessary to those in the class called executive.'

'Like the buildings invariably called "homes" by developers,' said Thrasymachus. 'In my day builders built *houses* and advertised them as such.'

Euthydemus ignored this and replied directly to Socrates. 'I get as far away from people as possible, in the solitary occupations of sailing and fishing.'

'What kind of boat, and how built, do you sail?' Socrates asked.

'A gunter-rigged Bermudan sloop.'

'Of fibre?'

'Certainly not, Socrates. Clinker-built, like all real boats.'

'So that, at least, is one area where you admire what is old. And where do you fish?'

'In a wonderful stretch of a wonderful river in a wonderful, bird-haunted area, the name of which could not be dragged from me by wild horses.'

'But which it is safe to conclude is in an as yet unspoilt part of the Suffolk countryside?'

'I must admit that it is so, Socrates.'

Socrates paused for a long time. Then he said 'It is clear that all of this company, however differing their interests, have in their mind a view of the Perfect Suffolk; that the notions of space, wide sky, history, a unique deposit of architecture both ecclesiastical and domestic, the sense of a landscape lovingly developed over many centuries of slow pastoral growth are all involved in this view; and that, as many more persons in this age of mobility become aware of it and attempt to share it, there is the unavoidable paradox that it will be correspondingly reduced. It is clear also that there must be a close companionship between persons qualified and paid as Planners of our entire country, free from all taint of special interest, and ordinary persons who wish to play some part in either realising or at least preserving it.'

At this Nicephorus, son of Nicias of Bury, said 'O Socrates, I must confess that I came with my father with the intention of saying before you all that the preservation of Suffolk was purely the concern of old men. But as I listened to you I realised that I too should one day be an old man, and that we too must have a view of the Ideal, the Perfect Suffolk, of which all the aspects of Suffolk which we now actually see are, for all their beauty, a mere reflection. But how may we all be sure of seeing correctly this Idea of Suffolk, where Justice (that is the harmonising of conflicting claims) and Beauty combine in the Form we should all seek?'

At this impetuous and moving declaration Socrates smiled. 'Perhaps by joining the Suffolk Preservation Society,' he said.

Index of Suffolk Churches

Grid references are to map on page 6

Index

All the places listed are in Suffolk, unless otherwise indicated.